From Good to Bad Bankers

"I have no hesitation in recommending Aristóbulo's book *From Good to Bad Bankers* as mandatory reading for all regulators and supervisors anywhere in the world. The book is full of pearls of wisdom based on years of hands-on experience and problem solving in banking regulation and supervision. What is most remarkable about Aristóbulo is his unwavering belief that good supervision is the essence of regulation. To quote him: 'While it is good that international regulators have focused strongly on boosting bank capital, less attention has been paid to supervision, asset evaluation and provisioning, which could prevent or reduce the number and size of crises, including their effective solutions. An analogy would be the focus on paying for a funeral rather than preventing the need for one in the first place.' His view that on-site intensive and if necessary intrusive supervision to evaluate the banks' asset value is absolutely true and is something supervisors should follow anywhere in the world. In emerging economies like India, the book has great relevance and being based on practical experience, supervisors in these countries will find they can relate to it. The style is easy to read and understand and this is a big bonus for these countries."
—Usha Thorat, *former Deputy Governor of the Reserve Bank of India*

"Bank regulators, bankers, investors, students of banking and bank regulation, and anyone interested in finance: run, don't walk, to get a copy of this book. With it, you get a seat at the table with one of the most experienced and wisest supervisors on the planet, and you get to learn some key lessons that will serve you well. The first chapter alone is worth the price and will help inoculate you against the 'viruses' that at times run rampant in the financial world."
—Jerry Caprio, *William Brough Professor of Economics and Chair, Center for Development Economics, Williams College, USA*

Aristóbulo de Juan

From Good to Bad Bankers

Lessons Learned from a 50-Year Career in Banking

Aristóbulo de Juan
Madrid, Spain

Translated by
Daniel Duffield
Madrid, Spain

This book was originally published in Spanish in 2017 under the title De Buenos Banqueros a Malos Banqueros. The original publisher was Marcial Pons.
ISBN 978-3-030-11550-0   ISBN 978-3-030-11551-7   (eBook)
https://doi.org/10.1007/978-3-030-11551-7

Library of Congress Control Number: 2018968424

Cover credit © MBPROJEKT_Maciej_Bledowski / iStock / Getty Images Plus

This Palgrave Macmillan imprint is published by the registered company Springer Nature Switzerland AG.
The registered company address is: Gewerbestrasse 11, 6330 Cham, Switzerland

Foreword

In the late 1980s, the World Bank began to review the lessons of financial development and discovered that commercial and policy-based banks were failing not just in the developing countries, but also in the advanced economies. More than 25 developing countries took action during the 1980s to restructure financial institutions that were distressed. Something was seriously wrong with development if the financial sector does not work properly. Accordingly, the Bank assembled a team under the leadership of then Chief Economist, Stan Fischer, to 'disseminate' the news and to prepare the World Development Report 1989, which was devoted to the theme, Financial Systems and Development.

The Report was prepared by Millard Long, the Division Chief in Financial Policy and Systems Division of the Research Department, with a team that included Yoon Je Cho, Dimitri Vittas and Barbara Kafka. As part of the preparatory work, research projects and seminars were held to draw experience from all over the world. I was lucky to be hired in October 1989 as part of the Division to study bank failure and restructuring experience. Amongst the team already in place was Aristóbulo de Juan, a distinguished banker from the Bank of Spain, who had deep understanding of bank insolvency and failure from both the commercial banking and supervisory sides. He led a fight against the then conventional wisdom of deregulation and consolidation as the panacea to solve banking crises. Instead, he strongly advocated for identifying and solving problems by mechanisms based on asset evaluation and real cash flows. He thus changed the World Bank approach to diagnose and treat problem systems and became very well-known at the Bank and in a variety of countries.

The 1989 Report was seminal because it revealed how financial crises have many causes, both micro and institutional and the result of policy mistakes, distorted interest rates and exchange rates, and political failure. The team that Millard Long led, aided by Alan Gelb (later Chief Economist, Africa), comprised some of the most illustrious thinkers and doers in the finance field. Millard himself went on to advise the financial sector reforms in Russia and Eastern Europe. Patrick Honohan became the Governor of the Bank of Ireland, using all that he learnt to turn around the Irish banking system in 2009–2015. Jerry Caprio went to Brown University, producing books on financial regulation and finance. Yoon Je Cho returned to Korea to advise several presidents and is today Korean Ambassador to the United States. Ross Levine led the work on why finance matters to growth and, later, why bad regulatory policies contributed to later crises. He is today at the University of California, Berkeley. Asli Demurgic-Kunt from Turkey is today Director of Research at the World Bank and helped build the financial development database set. Stan Fischer was to become Deputy Managing Director of the IMF, Governor of the Bank of Israel and Deputy Chairman of the Fed Board of Governors.

Working from different countries with different experiences, the intellectual atmosphere at that time was electric, with different people contributing to the huge debate on why finance matters. Much of the work produced at that time remains as important insights to the financial crises that unfolded in 1997 in Asia and ten years later in 2007.

Aristóbulo was a man of few words, but his article for the Division, 'From Good Bankers to Bad Bankers', was read widely throughout the World Bank and many emerging market countries where World Bank projects to help reform banking systems were taking place. He was clear on the role of bank mismanagement, bad accounting and efforts to cover up losses. Wherever he went, from Latin America to the former Soviet countries, he was listened to because he talked not only common sense, but also true insights from experience and wisdom, tinged always with humour and wit. He was the epitome of the distinguished Spanish gentleman, but upright, wise, a worldly philosopher and a loyal friend. At Aristóbulo's farewell party, when leaving the Bank, Millard Long, said: 'Aristóbulo's legacy is very important. Changing a large and bureaucratic institution is very difficult. But in little more than two years, he has changed the paradigms of a large and bureaucratic institution, the World Bank'.

Aristóbulo went back to Spain where, from his own practice, has advised governments and leading banks in over 30 countries. Later, when the Spanish banking system again went into crisis in 2008, following the European debt crisis, he was very persistent in warning the Bank of Spain against the danger of belated, half-way or illusory treatments. He remains very active to-day as an advisor, a writer and a lecturer.

Finally, as Aristóbulo celebrates his 87th birthday, he has brought out the collection of his writings in the form of a book that has been published in Spanish and English. I advised him to also publish his book in Chinese so that his readership would be broadened to one of the largest banking systems in the world.

This book is evergreen—meaning a classic that will help bankers, regulators and policymakers through the ages—because bank crises are inevitable as long as there are banks. Aristóbulo de Juan brings a wealth of experience as banker, regulator, academic and analyst who has seen many cycles of crisis, restructuring and revival, only to decay back into crisis. Full of wit and wisdom, this book shows how good bankers can become bad bankers through micro- and macro-decisions that allow them to slip across financial discipline into covering up the losses. Aristóbulo's 'double loss rule' is only one of the gems that can be found in this treasure trove of practical banking and regulation. This is a must-read for all aspiring bankers and regulators, if only to bring common sense and reality back from the fog of excessive technical jargon that plagues banking today.

Bank regulators and financial economists do not need masses of technical data and jargon derived from modern rules, such as Basel III, to understand that bad failure is due to bad culture, often worse politics at both the large and small, personal levels. If you read any chapter in this book, you will find insights and ideas on how to detect and then restructure problem banks.

I cannot recommend any other book in this field more seriously than this one.

Beijing, China   Andrew Sheng
December 2018

Foreword

Read This Book ... You Might Learn Something

Let me recommend that you approach this book with an open mind for its extraordinary explanation of banks and banking, and of the industry's complex transformation via crisis management and the rescue and regeneration of financial institutions. The ramifications of bank resolution are usually dire and rarely entirely predictable. Saving banks from the consequences of their own bad management need not be a reward for failure. Indeed, it should be rather an exercise in prudence to avoid perverse consequences for the economy as a whole, for depositors and especially for the taxpayer, as well as protecting against adverse impacts on payments systems and confidence in general. Bank rescues do not necessarily mean extricating bankers from their own mess, but are rather about defending the interests of third-party depositors, who have no hand in ropey governance.

The articles included in this anthology are presented in chronological order of writing, and they offer a summary of the very practical and soundly realistic lessons gleaned by the author, Aristóbulo de Juan, over the years of a lifetime in banking. He has added to this experience the fruits of his personal reflection to reach well-founded conclusions and to build up a handbook to help head off, or at least mitigate, future crises. I cannot say whether the best of this volume lies in the suggested diagnoses and their recommended treatments, or in the preventive proposals outlined in each of the articles it contains. Each, however, unerringly addresses its subject matter with tact and sensitivity.

The wide-ranging texts contained in this book (comprising speeches, articles and papers addressing a spectrum of different audiences) provide a critical yet orthodox vision of banking and, at the same time, a guide to do's and don'ts for both bankers and regulators alike. They will also appeal to lay readers interested in the logic of the banking industry and its effects on society as a whole for the light it sheds on what constitutes good and bad practice on the part of professional bankers and the nature of the business, which is as old as trade and as complex in detail as it is straightforward in its definition and nature, as well as supervisors, and indeed to anybody engaged in the regulation and oversight of the finance industry, not to mention politicians and legislators, who must often make critical decisions quickly and sometimes find themselves the prisoners of unfounded myths and legends.

The author is an old hand at this game. He came up through the ranks of the banking business and has worked both in the private sector and as a regulator, as he himself explains in his prologue, so I will not recount his career for the sake of brevity. Suffice it to say that Aristóbulo was a senior commercial banker at Banco Popular Español in the 1970s, when it was run by Luis Valls and was a byword for excellence. The Valls brothers would in fact themselves come to Aristóbulo from time to time to seek his help figuring Luis out. To this hands-on experience, Aristóbulo adds his roles as a crisis manager, a supervisor, an international consultant, a teacher and a disseminator of ideas, subject only to the dictates of his own personal criteria.

Having gained his spurs as a banker, Aristóbulo was asked by the Bank of Spain and the Spanish banking community to help manage the crisis that had engulfed some 50 Spanish credit institutions in the early 1980s, taking the supervisory authorities totally by surprise and highlighting their scant legal and financial baggage and lack of practical experience. It was time to improvise and invent, to take bold risks of a very unbureaucratic nature to address the crisis, which had erupted at a very difficult moment in Spanish politics. Meanwhile, the measures taken to rescue and regenerate ailing banks, and to return them to the market under new management and in the hands of new owners had to be explained both to the authorities and to Spanish public opinion.

Aided by his team, Aristóbulo diligently undertook this task with prudence and immense practicality, ensuring that all decisions were duly documented, avoiding any hint of high-handedness or grandstanding, and eschewing any condemnation with the benefit of hindsight. One of the burdens of crisis management is the risk that one will be judged on the basis of arguments and opinions that could not have been imagined while the search for solutions was on and critical decisions were being taken. 'Make sure you can explain whatever you do even years later and in a different context', a veteran banker once told him. Aristóbulo can explain it all because he managed to be both cautious and daring at the same time.

In a tribute when Aristóbulo left the Bank of Spain, the then Governor Mariano Rubio said, '[He] managed government money as if it were his own', while the minutes to the meeting of the bank's governing board held on the same day note, '[A]mong Mr. de Juan's qualities, two stand out above the rest—his capability, mettle and sheer courage in moments of difficulty above and beyond his technical stance, and his gift for finding effective solutions to combat the banking crisis. His drive and commitment were fundamental to the creation of the Inspection Department, which he leaves well trained and ready to keep up his own good work.'

Despite the lack of legal, financial and professional tools, the crisis of the 1980s was more than successfully resolved, leaving a legacy from which other countries have also benefitted. My own feeling, however, is that this cumulative experience was largely ignored in the handling of the current financial crisis. The collapse of the Spanish savings banks has ruined fully one-third of the country's financial system, which appeared to be in rude health just before the crisis broke, although financial channels, loan books and the ownership and management model were in fact already showing signs of strain, and problems were compounded by feeble and insouciant oversight. Between them, these factors first sparked the crisis and then stoked its costs.

The author worked out his anti-crisis strategy and methodology over the course of a long career. This book distils his conclusions, the fruits of reflection after action, on the management and prevention of banking crises, an objective that is vastly more important than merely assuring post-mortem financing.

Aristóbulo displays the reflective style of a methodical person, seeking to identify, analyse and understand problems as if they formed part of a puzzle laid out on his desk; to construct a discourse and to explore the complex and contentious decisions involved in the resolution of any crisis.

The first article, 'From Good Bankers to Bad Bankers', presented as Chap. 1, was published initially in 1986, although the ideas it contains were first sketched out in Aristóbulo's reports to the shareholders of crisis-ridden banks in the early 1980s, who were asked to approve the essential changes in management and 'accordion transactions' (capital reduction and increase) required to save the day. One of Aristóbulo's most important arguments is that banking crises, which recur with depressing regularity, are not an inevitable consequence of economic crisis or recession, but often caused by poor decisions that spiral down into an inferno of insolvency, passing through a first circle of 'bad management' to a second of 'cooking the books' then to a third of 'desperate measures' and so on until eventual collapse and outright fraud. The author offers reasonable, feasible solutions to avoid this nightmare descent. The rare fruit of this vision and experience is his four-line synopsis, which remains as valid today as it ever was.

The last article, 'Practical Lessons for Dealing with Problem Banks', presented as Chap. 12, was written this year and is a recapitulation of Aristóbulo's decades of experience. He presents the 'state of the art' in crisis management in 2017 while maintaining the basic ideas of the 1986 text. We now have fresh evidence regarding the closely related matters of 'regulation', 'supervision' and 'resolution' to suggest that the quality of the whole is determined by the weakest link.

Aristóbulo revisits some of the concepts he has coined since the 1980s, such as the metaphor of 'evergreen' loans to describe the kind of non-performing loans that are simply disguised so as to continue generating fictitious interest and present the appearance of solvency. Maintaining evergreen loans is like sweeping problems under the carpet. As the author shows, however, it eventually becomes necessary to take a new broom to a struggling bank if failure is to be avoided.

Another of the author's key propositions is the notion that losses are scaled by five multipliers—minor losses estimated by a bank's management; twice that amount according to a qualified audit report; losses calculated by the supervisor, which are once again twice the previous amount; again twice the amount after resolution; and finally, the losses identified by the institution's buyer/white knight, which are again usually twice the previous amount. This formula holds in all too many cases, and it forms part of the nature of banking that the recognition of liquidity problems points unswervingly to the reality of insolvency.

Perhaps the most valuable thing about this mature work, though at 86 Aristóbulo retains the mental capacity of a 50 year old, is the author's critique of the origins of the present crisis and of the international rules and institutions that have emerged from it. He believes the crisis is not over, and that there is still plenty of sweeping-up to be done. He argues that the prime cause of this crisis was excess liquidity, which is often a breeding ground of insolvency because it allows problems to be buried while reckless growth continues unchecked. Easy liquidity cannot cure the sickness but only provides a short-term breathing space, while the symptoms will only grow worse without unflinching surgery. There is also an underlying idea that insufficient provisioning of impaired assets reduces the incentive to dispose of them. Holding on to assets that do not produce real returns takes up scarce capital and only results in further losses. This a losing game played by losers.

I find the critical analysis of recent supervisory procedures involving mathematical modelling, external audits and stress testing very suggestive, given that these tools have neither produced the expected results nor prevented some very unpleasant surprises. Such 'unknown unknowns' conspire against the algorithms constructed on the basis of prior information. Meanwhile, the fashionable belief that enhanced governance could take the place of demanding supervision is shown to be no more than self-delusion.

Aristóbulo argues in favour of supervision in situ, sampling loan files to verify the reality of cash flows (interest, provisions, repayments and reserves) and whether the fair values of assets and credit returns are or are not in fact as recognized in the financial statements. He underscores that insolvency can be avoided, and must be resolved, using capital, whether in the form of cash contributions, actual retained earnings or current profits. Though it may be important to provide institutions with capital, it remains merely instrumental. If we hope to lighten the burden thrust upon the taxpayer, however, it is much more important to prevent insolvency in the first place by means of rigorous accounting and realistic measurement of assets than to reduce and/or increase capital after the event. The author stresses that earnings are key. He also warns against shortcuts to recapitalize anaemic entities with insufficient or low-quality equity. He believes measures of this kind to be a sham which only feigns a proper capital injection. Finally, he insists on the importance of 'fit and proper' professionals with the necessary experience and integrity to replace the managers of failed institutions.

In short, this is a very practical book, and its conclusions are both theoretically valid and backed by experience. Though Aristóbulo makes no academic claims, the empirical validity of his tried-and-tested findings is plain. Lucidly and precisely phrased by a skilled writer relying on his own wits and drawing on that wealth of common sense which is always available to a free and independent mind, the chapters themselves are a pleasure to read.

Madrid, Spain   Fernando González Urbaneja

Prologue

This book is a selection of articles I have written about banking and its pathologies over the course of 30 years between 1986 and 2017. The decision to publish them together was originally the idea of a good friend and colleague who insisted, when I at first refused, that it was time at this late stage in my banking career for me to set down my thoughts and observations in writing by way of a legacy. I have sought to avoid articles on overly topical themes, limiting my selection to writings which were not only of current interest when they were written but remain so today and may continue to be so in the future. This book has been planned as a small, straightforward volume for scholars, business schools, bankers and, above all, supervisors, a *vade mecum* based on experience rather than on long research among dusty tomes.

Having studied law and economics, I entered banking almost by accident back in 1963, and I am still here more than 50 years on. I have had the immense good fortune to have seen how our financial systems work from different yet complementary points of view. At the start of my career, I worked in merchant banking at Banco Popular Español when it was still led by Luis Valls-Taberner, and at the time it was an outstanding school of banking. After some years working as Assistant to Valls-Taberner in the management of the group's six banks and their affiliated financial firms, all of them sound, I was made CEO of Banco Popular. I rotated periodically through executive posts in almost all departments, which gave me the opportunity to participate actively in Banco Popular's modernization as it grew from a small, if venerable, local institution to one of the world's most profitable banks in the 1980s and 1990s. Meanwhile, I learned the principles of sound management almost by osmosis.

While I was CEO of Banco Popular, the Bank of Spain and the Spanish banking community asked me in 1978 to help resolve the looming banking crisis that would last until well into the 1980s. As a result, I remained in the orbit of the Bank of Spain for some nine years, spending the first half of this period as CEO of Corporación Bancaria, S.A., the bank's hospital as the press liked to call it, which eventually became the Spanish bank deposit guarantee scheme (*Fondo de Garantía de Depósitos*). For the second half of this period, I was assigned to the Bank of Spain's Directorate General (DG) for Inspection, today's DG Supervision, making me directly responsible for the supervision in situ of some 350 Spanish banks, savings banks and credit cooperatives. In this role, my team and I were able to identify and resolve some 60 insolvent banks masquerading as robustly profitable organizations. This task included the nationalization of the 20 Rumasa Group banks, a dramatic episode which I and the excellent professionals in my charge saw through under the strong leadership of various outstanding figures. The circumstances demanded radical decision-making, the creation of new tools and a willingness to take risks of all kinds. Restructuring was successfully achieved in the absence of asset valuation regulations or any further legislation than general company law.

This was a tremendous professional school for me personally. I learned more than I otherwise could have done of both good and (mostly) bad banking practice. In short, I learned what not to do. This mindset proved an extraordinary addition to what I already knew, and I have cultivated it avidly ever since.

After these nine eventful years, I was recruited by the World Bank, which had followed the Spanish crisis closely and wished to apply the principles and mechanisms used in its resolution internationally. In my three short years as a World Bank Financial Advisor, I visited and examined entire financial systems (and no longer just individual banks), recommending legislative reform and the creation of new supervisory tools to the governments of countries with grave problems, not all of whom were willing to change. With the tireless encouragement of my bosses, I also found time to write articles and speak at banking conferences and events. It was their desire that I should leave behind a legacy of ideas, not least for the use of the World Bank's own staff, which would help establish a series of 'ground rules' for regulation and realistic supervision to combat 'obscurantism' and ensure the practical effectiveness of bank rescue operations through restructuring and the sale of failed institutions so as to definitively resolve problems and prevent backsliding. I had graduated from the case-by-case diagnosis of individual banks' problems to the reform of financial systems as a whole, another milestone in my professional education.

Governments rarely accepted our advice and occasional demands wholeheartedly. However, I have often found, upon returning years later to the countries concerned, that our ideas had gradually permeated deeper than had initially seemed possible and now constituted a benchmark of good practice.

By way of an aside, I may say that my time at the World Bank completely changed my public image. Where I was initially seen as a member of Opus Dei, the result of my 15 years in the orbit of Banco Popular, my nine years in the orbit of the Bank of Spain had apparently made me a sympathizer of the Spanish Socialist Party in the eyes of many, particularly after the nationalization of the Rumasa Group. Though I am in no way ashamed of either of these alleged affiliations, neither image is entirely true. I have actually never been ideologically right or left wing, which I find blinkered. I saw myself simply as a professional committed to hard work wherever I might find myself at any given moment.

In late 1989, almost 28 years ago now, I decided that it was time to return to Madrid to share what I had learned and so I set up the consultancy which I still run in Spain's capital today.

Between my activity in Spain, my time at the World Bank and my consultancy engagements, I must have worked in banking systems on four continents. I have designed legislation, reformed supervisory regulations and mechanisms, drafted reports for banks and governments, and published no small number of articles and papers. I have also taught widely, speaking at seminars in leading universities, including several in the US and in the United Kingdom. I have also addressed conferences at the Federal Reserve and of course at the biannual Seminar for Senior International Bank Supervisors, which I helped bring about with the aid of the Federal Reserve, the IMF and the World Bank. This event started in 1988 and is still going strong today. Of course, I have also written numerous press articles on the financial crisis in Spain, although these more ephemeral writings do not appear in this volume.

The goal of my writing has always been to influence the ways in which managers run their banks and in which the authorities deal with financial problems.

This book contains a selection of complementary articles, which I believe have stood the test of time and remain relevant today. A brief summary of the subject matter of the book is as follows.

I begin by describing the sorry path too often trodden by bankers when they put off dealing with their problems, which leads only to creeping deterioration ending in some cases in insolvency and even outright fraud.

I then relate and analyse the Spanish banking crisis of 1978–1985 based on figures first collected in 1983, describing a series of mechanisms that have remained largely overlooked by other authors.

The next chapter describes a series of micro and management factors which are commonly found to trigger or aggravate crises.

I then go on to address the often-poisonous relationship between banks, bankers and their related companies, epitomized in the case of the socialist countries of Eastern Europe.

In the following chapter, I identify a series of situations which present serious obstacles to the successful handling of crises, even where sound regulatory and institutional structures exist.

I then go on to take a brief look at certain unethical practices and attitudes that I have found to be prevalent among bankers and supervisors in times of crisis.

Next, I denounce excess liquidity and headlong growth as the mainsprings of insolvency that they are.

I then go on to sketch out the formula I proposed in 2009 to address Spain's recent financial crisis, which began in 2007. This proposal was initially well received by the Bank of Spain, but was not finally applied for a number of very different reasons.

In this penultimate chapter, I identify some problems which have seriously impaired the functioning of the European Banking Union, and I again decry the pervasive unwillingness to address the problem of insolvency on the spurious grounds of financial and political stability.

Finally, I present a summary of the main lessons I have learned in my long years of professional practice.

In everything I have written, I have always endeavoured to highlight the differences between those regulatory tools and mechanisms that work and those that do not, and I have sometimes been accused of carping for my pains. The reason for this insistence is that ineffective measures tend to leave financial systems riddled with even costlier problems, which can seriously hurt the wider economy.

Why publish this book now? While many have concluded that the crisis is finally over, others like myself believe that we must keep up our guard at a time when the aftershocks are still being felt, when the prestige of the Bank of Spain has taken a bad knock and when Europe's Single Supervisory Mechanism is still struggling to make headway and has suffered some serious reverses. It also seems to me a good time to reflect, now that the aftermath of the crisis has had time to meld with the distortions, bubbles and moral hazard that are the side effects of the monetary policy followed by central banks the world over, raising the spectre of renewed financial turbulence.

How did this book get its title? Quite simply—it is the title of an article I wrote in Washington while convalescing from a knee operation in November 1986, when I had only recently arrived from the Bank of Spain. *From Good Bankers to Bad Bankers* it was, then as now. The original article appears as

Chap. 1 of this book. In it, I describe the slippery slope down which even a good banker may slide to ruin. This article had a major international impact on its publication and is still widely read today. Upon arriving in a country for the first time, at some point, one or other of the local notables will often say, 'Your name is very well known here.' If it is, it is for the article in question.

There were hardly any actual bankers in the World Bank in 1986. It was stuffed rather with infrastructure experts and capital market wizards. These colleagues listened to my reasoning with respect, but with some reserve. 'When you learn the reality of our countries, your ideas will change', they assured me.

It was then that I decided to set down in writing what I had experienced in Spain while it was still fresh in my memory to allow comparison with other countries, and that was the genesis of the article that now starts this book. Following my time at the Bank of Spain, I would go on to work in banks in some 30 countries between World Bank assignments and my own consultancy, and I have found that the phenomena of insolvency are actually very similar everywhere. My article remains current, then, even 30 years on.

It has been translated into ten languages and has made its way around the world. It is still considered essential reading and has been treated as a *vade mecum* for supervisors and regulators in various countries, and even in international institutions. Moreover, the basic concepts it contains resonate strongly through some of the other articles selected for this work.

How was I to end the book? One must choose the right end, as we see in film. I decided to offer an orderly synthesis of the practical lessons that I have learned in situ without referring directly to the articles selected here, even at the risk of repeating some ideas. This is the origin of the article entitled *Practical Lessons on the Treatment of Problem Banks*, which closes this short work. Spain is not mentioned. Still, a word to the wise … a paper on non-performing loans has been added, to describe the serious problem that affects European banking. To close the work, I have included my views presented to the Spanish Congress on our crisis.

In any case, I would not wish to end this prologue without mentioning some key features of this little compendium, which set it apart from most of the books published on the subject of financial crises and banking problems in general.

In the first place, none of the ideas set out here are the fruit of academic research or were prompted by the work and opinions of others. On the contrary, they are inspired solely by my own direct experience.

The approach I have taken in this book is radically empirical, the result of direct observation case by case, and my conclusions were reached mostly by inductive inference from the specific to the general. As the former Spanish minister of economy Miguel Boyer liked to say, it is the specific and the micro that feed the general and the macro (though nobody should expect to find broad macroeconomic ideas here).

Let me stress that my approach in this book is not merely technical, but also addresses the subject from a 'behavioural' standpoint, which seeks to understand the important role played by human nature, psychology and people's individual actions in business and, of course, in banking.

Finally, let me end with an anecdote which encapsulates the response to my writings. Sometime around 2000, I attended a major public event in Mexico City, where I had worked on occasion in an advisory capacity. While there, I ran into Ángel Gurría, then the Mexican Treasury Secretary and today a Director of the OECD in Paris. On seeing me he cried out in surprise, '*Hombre*, Aristóbulo! Our conscience!'

To sum up, this book is an anthology of my writings over the last three decades, structured in chronological order, and my aim in publishing it is to show that the phenomenology of the micro and institutional problems that lead to insolvency and financial crisis is practically identical in all countries, and is most likely to stay the same in the future. In my view, all of the articles selected have stood the test of time, as the reader will, I hope, observe in the concluding remarks of several chapters.

After four decades advising and helping governments address banking dilemmas in some 30 countries, I believe that my thinking on the salient issues, as reflected in these pages, remains as reasonable and valid today as it was when I started.

In making a compilation of this kind, it is of course necessary to respect the original articles selected for inclusion and to exercise editorial restraint. Though it may involve some repetition, this approach seems to me the lesser evil and, in any case, I believe that it is often instructive to insist on key ideas. Finally, I find that my ideas are still held in high regard by specialists in a number of world institutions, where some have treated them almost as a school of thought.

Madrid, Spain   Aristóbulo de Juan

Contents

1   From Good Bankers to Bad Bankers   1
  1   Introduction   1
  2   An Attempt to Define Management   2
  3   Technical Mismanagement   4
  4   The Crossroads   6
  5   Cosmetic Management   7
  6   Desperate Management   10
  7   Fraud   11
  8   A Few Lines on Management Culture Deterioration   12
  9   The Role of Banking Supervision   13
  10 Lessons to Be Learned   14

2   The Spanish Banking Crisis of the 1970s and 1980s   17
  1   Introduction   17
  2   Background to the Banking Crisis   17
  3   The Crisis and Its Causes   19
  4   Initial Approaches to Dealing with the Banking Crisis   21
  5   The Deposit Guarantee Fund   22
  6   Main Features of the Fund   23
  7   Operation of the Fund   24
  8   The Rumasa Case   26
  9   Results and Lessons Learned   28

3   **The Microeconomic Roots of the Banking Crises**   31
    1   The Roots of Banking Crises: Microeconomic, Supervisory
        and Legislative Issues   31

4   **'False Friends' and Banking Reform**   41
    1   'Good Friends' and Banking Reform   41

5   **The Dynamics of Undisclosed Insolvency**   53

6   **Obstacles to Crisis Resolution. Excerpts from the Paper**
    'Clearing the Decks'   57
    1   Obstacles to Crisis Resolution   57
    2   Some Remarks on Moral Hazard   62

7   **The Financial Systems and the Ethics of Restructuring**   67
    1   The Build-up to Crisis   68
    2   Let Us Now Turn to the Matter of Accounting Malpractice   70

8   **Liquidity and Euphoria**   77

9   **The Recommended Option**   81

10 **The Problems of the European Banking Union**   87

11 **Stability and Its Risks**   91

12 **Practical Lessons for Dealing with Problem Banks**   95
    1   Introduction   95
    2   Management   96
    3   Prudential Regulation   99
    4   Supervision   102
    5   Resolution   107

13 **Non-performing Loans: NPLs**   115
    1   Supervision   115
    2   Questionable Impressions   116
    3   Oft-disregarded 'Rules of Thumb'   116
    4   Mechanism for NPL Resolution   119

    5   Tightening the Screw   119
    6   Inspections, Provisions and Capital   120
    7   Remaining Questions   122

14 **Whys and Wherefores of the Spanish Crisis**   123
    1   Introduction   123
    2   The Origins of the International Crisis   124
    3   The International Bubble   124
    4   Why the Savings Banks?   126
    5   What About the Supervisors?   126
    6   The Case of Bankia   134
    7   SAREB   137
    8   Banco Popular   138
    9   The Cost to the Taxpayer   140
   10   The Situation Today (December 2017)   142
   11   Conclusions   143

Index   145

About the Author

Aristóbulo de Juan has dedicated his life to banking since 1964 in a career spanning more than 50 years, 13 of them as a senior executive in private retail banking and some 40 more as a front-line supervisor and consultant, dealing with bank reform and helping governments address financial crises on four continents.

After his time in retail banking, he spent nine years in the orbit of the Bank of Spain, initially as founder, Secretario General and CEO of *Fondo de Garantía de Depósitos*, the Spanish public-private deposit guarantee and restructuring scheme, and then as Director General of Supervision at the central bank itself. In these positions, he played a key role in the treatment and resolution of the Spanish banking crisis of the 1980s and in the modernization of Spain's supervisory mechanisms.

In 1986, he went on to spend three years as a financial advisor to the World Bank (WB) in Washington, where he led teams dealing with financial reform and crisis management in emerging economies, in the orbit of Vice President Stanley Fisher. He also advised top managers of the bank on the above areas.

In 1989, he set up his own consultancy firm specializing in banking, problem banks and bank supervision. From his practice, he has advised the largest Spanish financial institutions and the governments of 30 countries, including most Latin American ones, the US, China, Russia, Poland, Hungary, Turkey, Egypt, Argelia and Ghana.

He has lectured widely and participated in seminars at Oxford, Harvard, Yale and Wharton Business School, as well as in international organizations, such as International Monetary Fund (IMF), WB, Inter-American Development Bank (IDB), European Bank for Reconstruction and Development (EBRD) and Organization for Economic Cooperation and Development (OECD).

He has also lectured at central banks and/or bank superintendencies at the Federal Reserve Board (FED), China, Russia, India, Mexico, Perú and Colombia, as well as at the European Central Bank.

He has written numerous documents that were published by well-known publishers, such as Oxford, Elsevier, WB, IDB and EBRD. Most of these documents were widely disseminated in banking and supervisory circles worldwide. Some of them have been translated into several languages and are internationally considered as classics.

Since 2017, he contributes to the *Central Banking Journal* and is a member of the advisory board of the Spanish financial daily *Expansión*. He has written numerous articles on the financial crisis of 2007 and co-authored a book on the subject with Francisco Uría and Íñigo de Barrón, which was published in 2003 under the title *Anatomía de una crisis*.

In 2017, he was granted the 'Financial Excellence Award' for all of his banking career, by Instituto de Estudios Financieros (I.E.F.), a leading Barcelona-based foundation and business school.

List of Figures

Fig. 2.1   The Spanish banking crisis (1978–1984)   20
Fig. 2.2   Spain: financial restructuring   26
Fig. 5.1   Financial statements versus reality, an experiential model   55

1

From Good Bankers to Bad Bankers

Look, Mr de Juan, there isn't a bank in this country that isn't bust, but they all report profits and distribute dividends.
What's more, every Minister believes he owns one of our banks, and they're always ringing up.
The Governor of the Central Bank of a major Western nation, September 1987

When a bank is going well, its accounts are transparent. When it has problems, it will fiddle them away.
A. de Juan

1 Introduction

1. This chapter is not intended to be a rigid manual or pass any ethical judgement on bankers' behaviour. Rather, it is a model made up of features that repeat themselves historically around the world, both in developing countries and in developed ones.

2. Contrary to the theory that financial crises are only due to macroeconomic factors, this chapter stresses the role of bank management (not to mention ineffectual supervision) as a major element in all banking crises, and as a potential originator or multiplier of losses and economic distortions. It also stresses the fact that even good bankers, when in trouble, often become bad bankers, through a step-wise process of deteriorating attitudes.

First written as an internal World Bank working paper in 1986, this article went on to win an international audience and was translated into ten languages, including Russian and Chinese. It was co-published by the World Bank and Oxford University Press in 2002.

3. Poor management and ineffective supervision are relevant not only to the crisis of individual institutions, but also to widespread and systemic crises affecting all or most of a banking system. Of course, crises may also be caused by economic upheavals, inappropriate monetary or exchange rate policies and/or abrupt deregulation. In those cases, both good banks and bad banks can be found, depending on the quality of their management. In fact, good management may enable banks to survive and stay reasonably healthy in the midst of macro-problems. On the other hand, even in times of stability, bad management will lead to deeper crisis, by compounding losses, misallocating resources and contributing to inflation through high interest rates. Therefore, applying only macroeconomic remedial action to general financial crises, without simultaneously addressing their micro and institutional side, may prove ineffective or even counterproductive.

4. Banking supervision appears as a key element to prevent or limit the damage caused by poor management. The concept of supervision is used here to cover regulation, supervision proper and remedial action (from conventional enforcement to restructuring of institutions). If good regulation, supervision and remedial mechanisms are in place, bad management is less likely to exist. And if it exists, it is less likely to be deep and to last. Remedies can be put to work to stop and reverse deterioration. And because of the acceleration potential of deterioration, the sooner, the better.

5. The features of the model described and the lessons to be learned are merely sketched out in this chapter for the sake of simplicity.

2   An Attempt to Define Management

6. The above assertions make it important to analyse the managerial problems that lead banks to fail and to examine what regulations and supervision could do to prevent or remedy them.

7. Regulators in the US have a system to rate banks according to the quality of *c*apital, *a*ssets, *m*anagement, *e*arnings and *l*iquidity. They call it the CAMEL system, after the initials of those items. Each particular institution is given periodical marks by the supervisors, according to the performance in a series of aspects that make up each of those areas. Averages for each area and for the whole exercise are used to rate banks from 1 to 5, from very good to failing banks.

The elements used as a basis to rate an institution's management are as follows:

- competence
- leadership
- regulatory compliance
- ability to plan
- ability to react to changes in the environment
- quality of policies and ability to control implementation
- quality of management team
- risk of insider dealing
- succession prospects

A satisfactory response to those concepts might make a good definition of good management. If all banks were well managed, the only reasons for failure would be those due to the economic background. Even in those cases, the need for regulation and supervision would exist, in a similar way that traffic laws and policemen would be necessary even in a country of good drivers. Both banking and driving are risky activities for third parties.

8. Let us draw a picture of things that could certainly happen in the context of non-existent or ineffective regulation and supervision. Types of misman-agement can be grouped into four categories:

(a) technical mismanagement,
(b) cosmetic mismanagement,
(c) desperate management (*la fuite en avant*) and
(d) fraud

These do not have to occur in a sequential manner, though they often do. In fact, when technical mismanagement leads to losses or to the need for a dividend reduction, it frequently unleashes 'cosmetic' and 'desperate' management responses sequentially. Fraud may be a part of the process from the very beginning, but it is dealt with at the end, as a part of the dynamics that make good managers become bad managers. Illiquidity comes at the end of the process. In the meantime, the bank in question may have lost its capital several times over.

9. Whereas non-financial institutions may experience illiquidity despite underlying solvency, a peculiarity of banking is that *insolvency invariably precedes illiquidity*. The dimensions of their portfolios, the leverage banks operate with and their ability to raise money by offering high rates of return and publishing fictitious financial statements are the key differences between financial and non-financial firms.

3   Technical Mismanagement

10. Technical mismanagement may occur

(a) when a new bank is set up under new managers who are not 'fit and proper';
(b) when control of an existing bank is acquired by new owners; and
(c) when an existing bank that used to be well managed proves unable to plan ahead for changes or fails to acknowledge and honestly report a deteriorating situation, and to remedy it.

11. Technical mismanagement may involve a whole variety of inadequate policies and practices. The most relevant ones are overextension, poor lending, lack of internal controls and poor planning.

12. *Overextension and quick growth* are some of the major sources of failure. Overextension means lending sums of money that are not in proportion to the bank's capital, which is to say its cushion against potential losses. It may also mean diversifying activities to geographical or business areas the bank is not familiar with or is not well equipped to manage. Overextension is often connected with seeking *growth for the sake of growth, a typical banker's syndrome.*

13. *Poor lending policies* are a key danger that may also prove fatal. The key element of bank management is to make sure that deposits, which do not belong to a bank but to its depositors, are lent in such a manner so as to yield a proper return and are recovered by the bank. Policies or practices to avoid are:

(a) *Risk concentration.* This means making loans representing a high proportion of the bank' s capital to one single borrower or group of borrowers or to a given sector or industry. This practice may be the result of the free will of the banker (who believes in the eternal health of a given borrower) or the result of irresistible pressure from borrowers on the banker when they are unable to service their debt or even pay their operational overheads. Risk concentration is frequently mixed with connected lending, as described below. Not all concentration leads to failure, but most bank failures are the result of serious loan concentration.

Connected Lending This means a situation where the bank lends money to companies owned or controlled (totally or partly) by the banker or by the bank. Since ownership, especially in the case of bankers, is frequently indirect (through other subsidiaries or through decision-making relationships), the concept of connection is used rather than ownership, because of its wider connotation. Lending to borrowers connected to the bankers, beyond certain limits, is often fraudulent, as will be explained later in this chapter. In most cases, this kind of lending involves a high risk, because of the banker's tendency to use the bank as an instrument to finance his business, irrespective of its ability to repay, and to concentrate large proportions of the bank's lending on them. Concentration, default and permanent roll-over of loans are very common with connected lending. Most bank failures are also the result of connected lending. Lending to borrowers owned by the banks is typical of state-owned banks, including development banks. As a matter of principle, borrowers should be treated as if they were ordinary third parties. Scattered ownership and proper internal controls are significant elements to this effect. In practice, however, even if connected lending is limited to bank's subsidiaries, the danger exists that

(i) loans will be made according to less rigorous criteria and will concentrate a high proportion of capital, because of the parental relationship between the bank and the subsidiary;
(ii) the managerial attitudes of the subsidiary's directors will deteriorate because of their easy and systematic access to credit;
(iii) the bank's representatives on the subsidiary's board will develop a cosy relationship with the subsidiary and the people they are supposed to supervise, becoming an obstacle to information and control rather than a proper channel for both; and
(iv) the parent bank will seldom recognize a loan to a subsidiary as overdue or doubtful. Besides, in the case of state-owned development banks, short-term social objectives and political pressure may lead to bad loans and losses, whether or not accounted for in the books.

(b) *Mismatching.* This occurs when banks lend at terms that are out of line with the terms of their liabilities. Transforming terms forms part of the essence of banking, because money is fungible, and deposits may stay longer with the bank than their legal terms would suggest. But, when the terms of lending are overstretched far beyond those of liabilities or became so because of forced rollovers, serious *liquidity problems* may arise. Even if a bank that mismatches its assets and liabilities is able to solve the liquidity situation with interbank funding, it may have had to pay excessive rates for its new funding. And, if it operates with fixed interest rates, it may incur losses in the transformation. That is a modality of what is called *interest risk*.

One problem which can also prove particularly serious is mismatching of foreign currency exchanges.

(c) *Ineffective recovery.* This frequently stems from conflict of interest between the bank and companies owned by the bank or the bankers, as well as from political pressure on bankers or potential labour problems.

14. *Lack of internal controls* may also happen in different areas, but the most dangerous ones are those affecting

- *initial credit analysis and subsequent review procedures* which should be in place to avoid overly optimistic loans, excess risk concentration, inappropriate evaluation and rescheduling as opposed to timely recovery action;
- *information systems*, which should enable management to promptly analyse the trends of its business, and flash red lights as a warning of impairment or problems that can be addressed at an early stage; and
- *internal audits*, which should ensure that both regulations and internal policies are properly applied throughout the bank.

15. *Poor planning.* The ability to foresee is a very rare gift, but it can be developed with adequate techniques. However, poor planning is not only a matter of technique, but a matter of attitude. It is closely related with the *age* and/or vested interests of top management, with the *absence of teamwork*, and with the wishful thinking that banking *has always been a very safe business that needs no sophistication or adaptation to change.* 'We have always done very well', 'Nothing serious ever happens' and 'Problems are solved by time' are typical attitudes. In a context of economic upheaval, growing competition, financial 'menageries' and so on, it is easy to understand the consequences of poor planning. On the contrary, if a bank follows its own trends closely, if it tries to capture what is ahead in the economy and in the markets, it can adapt its strategy early so as to suffer limited damage and survive even in the midst of serious turmoil. Together with quick growth and bad lending policies, this aspect of mismanagement is the most frequent cause of bank deterioration.

4   The Crossroads

16. As a result of technical mismanagement and/or other macro- or micro-factors, a bank may find itself *in a situation where equity is increasingly eroded* by hidden losses, *real profits decrease* (if not disappear) and *dividends*, of course, *are in danger.* This would be the typical situation where good supervision or a good board would have the bank declare the real situation, change manage-

ment and inject new capital. Though such deterioration can be stopped, the lack of proper supervision and/or upright management leads to a very different situation. A drop in dividends is the key signal for the market that the bank is deteriorating and many bankers will tend to do everything in their power to avoid lack of confidence and to keep control of ownership and management. *This is the crossroad.* If the supervisor or the banker does not take the right road, the bank is doomed to become engulfed by 'cosmetic management' and 'desperate management', either one after the other or simultaneously. Management will get increasingly worse, the culture of the organization will deteriorate very quickly, the market will be distorted and a spiral of losses will soar. That is probably the point of no return. From then on, liquidation or restructuring is the only effective solution to a situation of insolvency that may grow in geometric progression.

5   Cosmetic Management

17. What may be called '*cosmetic management*' consists of hiding past and current losses so as to buy time and remain in control, while looking and/or waiting for solutions.

18. While there are almost infinite ways to hide the economic reality of a bank, some of them can be grouped in a model: the '*upside-down income statement*' technique. In a typical income statement, the first item is interest income and the last one is dividends, which are the result of adding and deducting all of the items in between. But when dividends are in danger, the banker may decide that they cannot be considered a variable, but a fixed element, that is taken as a basis to construct the remainder of the income statement down the ladder, through the manipulation of figures, no matter what the reality is. The 'upside-down income statement' would therefore tend to read as model A, as against a standard one, as shown in model B (Table 1.1).

19. In Model A, once *dividends* have been *predetermined*, the first area a banker will touch upon in order to maintain the same dividends is *undistributed profits*. This is not yet an accounting gimmick, but the threshold to cosmetics. The bank is sacrificing its equity capital for the sake of a 'good image' that no careful analyst should believe. Still, investors will receive the remuneration they were accustomed to.

20. The next problem arises when a further reduction in undistributed profits is no longer possible. Then, the banker will think of *manipulating net profits* in order to increase them on paper, even if that means having to pay more taxes. How? The banker will have four main resources to achieve his purpose:

Table 1.1 Upside-down income statement

Model A (upside down)	Model B (classic)
Dividends	Interest/income
+ Undistributed profits	- Financial cost
+ Taxes	= Spread
= Net profits	+ Fees
+ Provisions	- Overhead expenses
+ Sundry income/expenditure	= Operating profit
= Operating profit	+ Sundry income/expenditure
+ Overhead expenses	- Provisions
- Fees	= Net profit
= Spread	- Taxes
+ Financial cost	- Undistributed profits
= Interest income	= Dividends

(a) to provision less than required, through 'evergreening' procedures, or collateralization;
(b) to consider uncollectable accruals as income;
(c) to revalue assets; and
(d) to advance income accruals and postpone the accrual of expenditures.

21. '*Evergreening*'. The most serious problems of a bank are not in loans classified as overdue, which tend to be smaller loans that are being dealt with. *The worst losses of a bank are hidden* in the portfolio that is classified by the banker as *current portfolio* or 'good portfolio'. This means that when a banker wants to adapt provisions to a given level of profits and dividends, he will not classify a bad loan as overdue, doubtful or a write-off. Instead, he will automatically reschedule the loan over long periods of time, which will avoid classifying it as overdue. Interests will be refinanced. This is a snowball process that may lead to disaster because those loans become more and more difficult to collect and the borrower's bargaining position is strengthened because of the bank's failure to take effective recovery action. The culture of non-payment develops. Those practices are very typical of loans to companies where the bank or the bankers have stock, or where the bank has concentrated disproportionate sums of money.

22. Another typical way of reducing the need for provisions is to make a bad loan look good by obtaining collateral, even if it is economically insufficient to cover the debt or is impossible to foreclose on. For instance, loans with prior mortgages, factories with ongoing business and labour problems, real estate with limited or no development potential. However, the banker will account for the collateral as being worth the principal plus the interest to be accrued over a period of time. The borrower will again be very happy about it.

23. Even so, the borrowers may still have negative equity, current losses or even negative cash flow, but the bad banker will argue to the effect that he does not have to provision those loans, and that time will solve the stressed situation of the borrower. He may even go as far as to say that he 'cannot make provisions' for those and other bad loans, beyond the limits the tax laws consider as expenditure. 'Therefore', those loans are not bad.

24. The practices described above not only lead the banker to provision less than he should, but will also lead him to capitalize interest, that is, to account for refinanced interest (which in fact will be increased losses) as income. So, looking back to the income statement, the banker has achieved better 'profits' not only because provisions are lower, but even more important, because interest accruals are artificial, thanks to procedures that make loans look like 'evergreens'.

25. Suppose that 'evergreening' is not enough to keep profits at the desired level. The banker still has a way out, which is to revalue fixed assets, be they real estate or stock. Some legislation permits banks to periodically restate their assets in times of inflation without additional tax implications.

Some banks use this advantage to increase the book value of their assets beyond their economic value, thus creating artificial additional income (the difference between the previous book value and the new one) and reserves (as a counterpart of the asset revaluation).

26. Worst of all, some bankers may revalue their assets by selling them to companies that are connected with the bank, on credit, for a price above the book value, and account for the positive differences as income. The negative difference will not appear on the buyer's balance sheet as it should. Another type of 'revaluation' occurs when banks receive foreclosures that are insufficient to cover the loan in question but account for them at the loan value.

27. Another type of manoeuvre to hide losses is to advance the accrual of income and postpone accrual of expenditures. Let us mention a couple of examples. Fees should normally be spread over the term of a transaction. However, bankers in trouble will account for them the very day the fee is received. On the expenditures side, the banker may postpone accounting for commitments (for example, the payment of the price of a purchase) to the time of actual payment, instead of making the entry on the day the contract is signed.

28. Another common way of concealing losses is to recognize income based on accruals (rather than based on collection, even where this is actually doubtful) and expenses based on payment (rather than on the accruals basis), bringing recognition forward in the former case and deferring it in the latter.

6   Desperate Management

29. 'Desperate management' is an expression intended to describe a situation where bankers see themselves in danger of 'having to declare' a capital loss or having to pay fewer or no dividends. At that stage, the banker, besides indulging in cosmetics, will also look for business which may permit him to buy time, and if lucky, make up for the previous deterioration. The main practices followed when such attitudes take hold are

(a) speculation,
(b) paying rates above market rates for deposits, and
(c) charging high interest rates to borrowers.

30. When a distressed economic environment, bitter competition, and/or technical mismanagement lead to current losses and a high proportion of non-performing assets, the banker will look for alternative sources of income, most of the time, speculative activities. A few typical examples would include buying or financing real estate in times of inflation, in the hope that prices will keep increasing forever and a profit will be made when the property is sold; buying land as a basis for real estate development through loans from the bank; or buying stock under the assumption that you are making a short-term profit. Frequently, profit does not materialize because of a change in the market trends or because of inaccurate estimates. Think of a situation where a tight monetary policy brings in deflation and adjustment, the market becomes narrower and the value of real estate drops dramatically.

31. One particularly serious practice is the ongoing concentration of risks in problem clients who have already been granted large loans, not necessarily in the hope of recovering the amounts due but rather of saving the client from bankruptcy, which in many cases would also render the bank itself insolvent. This practice causes enormous distortions both in banks themselves and in the financial system as a whole.

32. What happens over the course of this process is that the bank's proportion of non-performing assets becomes higher and higher while providing no return. Therefore, the overall yield (which is supposed to cover deposits, interest payable and overheads) continues to diminish and new current losses grow, even if they go unreported. No matter how the cosmetics are applied and what the books show, the problem is now the real cash flow, which is impaired, and the bank begins to experience liquidity difficulties.

33. When in liquidity difficulties, the banker will go out to the market and offer very high interest rates to potential depositors and creditors. He needs to maintain an image of growth, he hopes that he can charge similarly high interest rates to borrowers and have growth absorb problems. Above all, he is just in need of cash. What for? In order to cover interest due to his depositors and even to be able to pay salaries and other fixed expenditures. Thus, the principal on deposits and facilities may no longer be entirely allocated to making new loans, but to pay and cover overheads. At this stage, the banker is taking funds knowing they are unlikely to be repaid to depositors. We are entering the area of fraud.

34. To the extent that the banker can still make new loans with a part of his deposits and credit, he will try to make up for the high remuneration he pays to creditors by charging above-market interest rates to his own borrowers. What happens is that he is now involved in a perverse process, because the quality of borrowers who will accept high interest rates is not likely to be the best. They are, typically, cases of stressed borrowers or of borrowers connected to the bank or the bankers, who hope they will not have to service their debt. The borrowers have negative equity. The connected borrowers have connections. Through this practice, the banker may have high spreads on paper in the income statement, but this will not be reflected in cash flows.

7   Fraud

35. Fraud may have been one of the causes of losses for a bank at an earlier stage. This is frequently the case when a bank is set up or acquired by speculators or businessmen having their own business interests. Also, fraud is involved in 'cosmetic' management, to the extent that it is a way of hiding the truth from the public in a business that is based on confidence. However, fraud is dealt with here at the end of the process, in order to suggest that a former good manager may become a fraudulent manager, through a deterioration process, such as the one described in this chapter. In fact, when illiquidity approaches and the banker feels the end may be near, he may feel the temptation to divert money out of the bank. The most typical channel is self-lending, that is, lending to companies that are owned by or connected with the banker. This may be done through special formal procedures that would make it very difficult for the bank to foreclose on him when he is no longer there. Another fraud which is typical of this last-minute situation is 'swinging ownership' of assets that are owned by the bank or the banker. If an asset is good, the banker may buy it from the bank at a low price. If an asset owned by the banker is in poor

shape, the banker will have the bank buy it from him at a high price. Of course, all such transactions will be 'properly' materialized through fiduciaries, paper companies, and other similar methods, so as to escape supervision. After all, the banker is in charge and 'It's all the Government's fault anyway.'

8   A Few Lines on Management Culture Deterioration

36. Deterioration of the management culture is one of the consequences of keeping problems unsolved as well as a source of long-lasting problems. The attitudes and example of top management permeate middle management and the lower layers of the organization. A bad management culture is very difficult to change. Changing a deteriorated culture may take a new management as long as it took the culture to deteriorate unless, of course, swift action is taken to renew several tiers of management at once. This is one of the reasons why change of ownership is advocated as one of the solutions to crises. Some features of a deteriorated management culture are as follows:

- Paper is mistaken for facts. Figures are mistaken for money. Hiding and cheating become normal. Even 'ethical'.
- Speculators become the ideal kind of managers to recruit or promote, since speculation becomes the ideal business, as one of the few hopes for recovery.
- Promotion of managers is based on loyalty, not on competence. Management information and teamwork disappear gradually.
- Internal audit activities are cut or confined to the investigation of minor problems in branch offices.
- Branch managers become 'one-legged professionals'. They receive instructions from their superiors to concentrate on the collection of deposits and stop lending, since all lending gradually concentrates in the bank's headquarters and main branch office.
- The fact that money is the raw material of the bank and the 'need for prestige' lead to inflation in staff, salaries and overheads. Luxury premises become a rule.
- As a counterpart of the culture of non-payment among borrowers of banks in distress, the bankers develop the culture of non-recovery.

9   The Role of Banking Supervision

37. The series of practices described under 'cosmetic management', 'desperate management' and fraud may be simultaneous or sequential. They can take place quite easily in countries where there is no proper regulation that makes them illegal or subject to remedy. But even if regulation is there, lack of adequate supervision may provide an ideal ground for them to take place and persist for a long time. This chapter does not elaborate on the rationale for banking regulation and supervision as a whole or on the key topics and activities involved in those concepts, but a few examples will be given below, regarding mismanagement aspects that could be prevented, limited or remedied:

(a) If entry into the market is regulated and supervised, that is to say, if a supervisory institution (the Central Bank or Superintendency of Banks) is able to control how to become a banker (setting up a new bank or buying control of an existing one), the danger for bank mismanagement may be considerably reduced.

(b) If a bank is required to send meaningful periodic information to the supervisory authority, including the balance sheet and income statement, analysis of that information would permit the bank itself and the supervisor to identify trends and the problems, and to take remedial action at an early stage, whenever necessary.

(c) If banks are required publicly to disclose their accounts in a reasonable disaggregated form, stockholders and the public will press management for remedial action, without the need for any public intervention.

(d) If the bank's accounts and assets are required to be audited by rigorous external auditors and their report is required to be sent to the supervisor and even published, this kind of verification would make hiding more difficult.

(e) If the legislation establishes rules that limit loan concentration, as well as connected lending, to a given proportion of capital, and if compliance is properly verified by the supervisor, the major risk of insolvency would be barred.

(f) If a minimum level of real equity capital versus assets is set, overextension and protracted undercapitalization would be limited risks.

(g) If rules are set for the bank to properly classify its assets as good or bad, and provisional and accrual recognition requirements are met, again with adequate verification by the supervisor, the state of health of the bank can be closely followed up and remedial action can be taken in due time.

(h) If proper penalties are established for mismanagement, lack of compliance with regulations or fraud, such as fines, replacement of management or legal action, the room for mismanagement would again be limited.
(i) Last but not least, if proper mechanisms were in place to facilitate bank closure and restructuring, the deteriorating situations could be stopped in time, avoiding spirals of market distortions and losses, that, in the end, will have to be covered by someone, most probably by the State.

10   Lessons to Be Learned

38. Many of these lessons are expressed or implicit in the foregoing text, but the risk of repetition is worth running for the sake of synthesis. So, a brief summary can be established below.

39. Regulation and supervision are not panaceas, but they are necessary pillars to have a strong financial system and limit damage caused by mismanagement and make macro-policies effective.

40. Good regulation and supervision may prove no good if there are no mechanisms in place to solve insolvency cases. This situation may even lead to corruption of the supervisor, who, for lack of remedies, may find himself forced to tolerate hiding.

41. Bad management is an essential ingredient of all banking crises. Only in cases of complex economic upheaval can a good management be overwhelmed by the context, but even in this case, there are good managers and bad managers. Good managers can limit the damage to a considerable extent.

42. The quality of management is dynamic. Once a bank has lost a significant part of its equity, a rapid process of deterioration is likely to take place unless the necessary changes are made to the institution's management and fresh capital is injected.

43. Losses are bound to multiply when bad management takes root, not only because of the need to plug existing financial holes but also because a deteriorating business culture that is riddled with unprofessional conduct and malpractice will only wreak further ruin.

44. Requiring minimum levels of equity does little to help unless adequate systems for the classification of assets, recognition of provisions and suspension of interest accruals are established and enforced.

45. The overdue and bad loans recognized as such on a bank's balance sheet tend to be negligible in solvency terms compared to large, unrecoverable loans that continue to be classified as current. The larger an unrecoverable loan,

in fact, the more likely it is that it will be recognized as current. If it were not, the banker would only uncover more serious problems.

46. Hence, loan restructuring and roll-overs are ideal for concealing losses, and they also provide the best means of reflecting fictitious equity and income in the accounts, because they do away with the need for provisions and allow unpaid accrued interest to be treated as revenue.

47. By using the practices described above to conceal problems and paying high rates of interest on deposits, an illiquid bank can keep going for a surprisingly long time, gradually losing its equity several times over. In other words, when illiquidity finally overtakes an institution, it will actually be in a situation of profound insolvency, which may have consumed not only its own equity but also a significant part of its borrowings.

48. The identification of losses and their recognition in the books may cause problems, but it can also work miracles if pressure from the market and the bank's own corporate bodies trigger timely corrective measures without the need for intervention by the authorities.

49. This is particularly important in the case of state-owned banks, where the loss of equity may be considered a less serious problem. In such cases, the identification and transparent reporting of losses is essential. Taxpayers' money is at stake, and proper public recognition of the situation may make not only bank executives more cautious but also politicians.

50. Bankers and politicians are often tempted to view all financial crises as being caused by factors inherent in the overall system and/or macroeconomic conditions. This stance provides bad bankers with an excellent argument to lobby for economic policy measures which suit them, or to demand government subsidies to save their businesses. Meanwhile, it offers politicians an excuse to apply only macroeconomic remedies in an effort to save everybody without creating any enemies, or even worse, to sit back and do nothing.

51. The ruinous consequences of deteriorating management described above, and the ongoing impairment of equity when a distressed bank avoids action to address its own illiquidity are factors that demand a swift response given the likelihood that the institution is already insolvent. Otherwise, losses will only increase exponentially while new deposits are applied not to profitable new business, but to shore up transactions that have no future. This is a danger not only for the institution itself, but for the whole of the financial system.

Note

This chapter was written in November 1986 and it is based entirely on the lessons learned by the author when he led the team that handled the Spanish banking crisis of the 1980s. However, its tenets have since proved applicable to problem banks later dealt with by the author in some 30 different countries between the time of writing and the publication of this book.

Its continued relevance is evident from the recent case of Banco Popular in Spain, which was a top-ranking European institution and a benchmark for many during the 1980s and 90s, but was eventually resolved by the European Banking institutions in 2017 following a process of deterioration that had started in 2004, when the bank's top management changed, making it the prototype described here 31 years before its resolution.

2

The Spanish Banking Crisis of the 1970s and 1980s

There was no crisis in Spain. You and our Governor just made it up to change the financial system and switch the bankers.
A senior executive of the Bank of Spain, 1986

1   Introduction

The Central and Eastern European Countries (CEECs) are very different from Spain. They have different financial systems and different bank supervision arrangements. The state of their economies and their banks is also different. Still there are many lessons, both financial and institutional, that could be learned from the successes and failures of the Spanish experience in dealing with its banking crisis between 1978 and 1984. The focus of this chapter will be on one of most important aspects for the CEECs of the Spanish case, notably the mechanisms that were put in place to rehabilitate problem banks.

2   Background to the Banking Crisis

When the banking crisis began in the late 1970s, the Spanish financial system was made up of 347 institutions. Of these, 116 were banks, including 106 private banks, 6 state-owned development banks and 4 subsidiaries of foreign

---

Address given at the International Monetary Fund (IMF) on 5 July 1985 as part of its first International Seminar on Problem Banks, marking the start of the IMF's activity in the field of banking. The seminar was attended by supervisors from numerous different countries and was chaired by Henry Wallich, Governor of the Federal Reserve Board.

© The Author(s) 2019
A. de Juan, *From Good to Bad Bankers*,
https://doi.org/10.1007/978-3-030-11551-7_2

banks. In addition, Spain had 80 savings banks and 151 credit unions, most of them engaged in lending to agriculture.

The central bank, the Bank of Spain, is responsible for supervising these deposit institutions. It is also the bank of issue and the lender of last resort.

Until the early 1970s, Spanish banking policy was characterized by a regulatory framework covering virtually all aspects of the deposit institutions' activities. Under this framework, the establishment of new banks was strictly limited, and the opening of offices was subject to a complicated maze of bureaucratic authorizations. There was, for several decades, a de facto prohibition against foreign banks entering the market. Interest rates were subject to ceilings which affected almost all deposits and a sizeable number of lending operations. At the same time, financial institutions, especially savings banks, were subject to a burdensome system of mandatory investment ratios designed to ease public sector financing and to promote exports, housing and a long list of other activities deemed as high priority.

The existence of a stringent set of prohibitions, restrictions and controls contrasted, however, with the wide scope of action enjoyed by banks in certain crucial areas, notably concentration of risks and bank solvency in general. This was due in large part to shortcomings in specific regulations or ineffective monitoring of existing guidelines.

The combination of a legal system which protected deposit institutions and a long period of economic prosperity (1960–1973) produced a complacent atmosphere in the banking system as high profit levels appeared to be guaranteed. However, the regulatory framework was eventually liberalized and some banks began to ignore the classic rules of banking prudence. In addition, the profitability of the banking sector had enticed a number of inexperienced entrepreneurs into banking, who began to control a number of small and medium-sized banks, taking advantage of the gaps in a control apparatus that was more imposing than it was effective.

It was within this overall framework that three important phenomena occurred in the 1970s.

First, there was the economic crisis brought about by the increase in oil prices which, in the case of Spain, rapidly brought the earlier phase of prosperity to a halt. In view of the political transition taking place in the country in the mid-1970s, it was not possible to adopt the necessary corrective action at the outset.

Second, and largely as a result of the economic crisis, huge budget deficits were incurred in the latter years of the decade, which grew even larger in the 1980s.

Finally, in the 1970s but notably beginning in 1974, the financial system was swept up by a strong wave of liberalization, which fundamentally affected the way banks did business. The new measures included broad scope for opening new bank branches and, in particular, they opened up the Spanish banking system to foreign competition as some 40 foreign banks received authorization to operate in Spain. Deposit interest rates and many lending rates were deregulated, making it possible to develop attractive new savings instruments. This proved very successful, with the foreign banking sector taking the lead in the development of new products. At the prompting of the Bank of Spain, a money market was developed, which was originally intended exclusively for banks. This change significantly reduced the impact of the mandatory investment ratios, especially for the saving banks.

3   The Crisis and Its Causes

In the context of this new more competitive environment, a serious banking crisis emerged, affecting a significant number of small and medium-sized banks as well as some savings banks and credit unions, equivalent in size to small banks. Out of a total of 110 private banks operating in Spain in the mid-1970s, 52 were affected by the crisis, holding deposits worth about $11 billion, over 20% of total deposits in the system. (Figure 2.1 shows the main features of the banking crises.)

While increased competition in the banking sector did nothing to make life easier, it was not in itself the principal cause of the banking crisis. In fact, the major banking groups, comprising the well-managed independent banks and most savings banks, weathered the storm of this competition quite nicely, maintaining sound positions and highly satisfactory profits.

Rather, the crisis affected those banks which

1. were closely tied to business groups to which they had made unwise loans, ignoring sound, basic banking practices;
2. had concentrated their risks in other banks; and
3. took highly speculative risks, notably in real estate development. These three factors were present in all banks that experienced difficulties. It is no accident that the 'industrial' banks, a category of institutions created in the 1970s to specialize in long-term and investment operations, were particularly affected.

The downturn in the general economic climate also revealed the financial weakness of some companies and brought an end to many poorly planned

YEAR	NUMBER OF BANKS TREATED	DEPOSITS & CREDITS IN MILLION DOLLARS (1)			NUMBER OF ACCOUNTS (IN THOUSANDS)	NUMBER OF BRANCHES	STAFF
		DEPOSITORS	CREDITORS	TOTAL			
1978	4	245	145	390	185	120	1,977
1979	2	214	51	265	201	61	1,026
1980	9	1,361	325	1,686	775	371	6,553
1981	4	564	294	858	362	151	2,143
1982	11	3,415	872	4,287	1,829	726	10,761
1983	21	4,859	1,686	6,545	1,946	1,193	13,204
1984	1	270	16	286	110	33	625
TOTAL	52	10,928	3,389	14,317	5,408	2,655	36.289 (2)

(1)   AT 175 PESETAS - 1 DOLLAR (1984 RATE)

(2)   100.000 APPROXIMATELY, INCLUDING STAFF IN NON-FINANCIAL SUBSIDIARIES

Fig. 2.1 The Spanish banking crisis (1978–1984)

deals, which could only have been maintained on the crest of the earlier wave of prosperity. It penalized those banks which, blinded by the ease of doing business in more prosperous days, had lent heavily to such companies without regard to financial prudence. Inevitably, many banks aggravated their situation by desperately competing to attract new deposits, either by paying interest rates well above market levels or by increasing their overheads (staff and offices) out of all proportion to their real business. It must also be stressed, however, that the difficulties experienced by a fair number of banks were attributable neither to conventional mismanagement nor to the adverse economic climate, but rather, to the fact that the interests of the banks were subordinated to the business objectives of their owners.

When the banking crisis erupted in late 1977, Spain did not have the legal mechanisms to rehabilitate banks, nor did a well-equipped supervisory apparatus or adequate prudential regulatory guidelines exist. When the first banks began to experience difficulties, there was really very little that could be done, short of improvising ad hoc solutions while at the same time introducing new and more permanent measures.

After examining the various possible alternatives, three primary options emerged:

1. let each institution solve its own problems as best it could;
2. close down those that could not; or
3. set up a system to protect depositors.

Experience indicated that, except in a few isolated cases concerning very small banks, it would be advisable to opt for rehabilitation and continuity. Due to the special nature of banking, a crisis in one financial institution can spread rapidly to another, producing a systemic problem, which may ultimately do serious damage to the general economy, as well as undermining international confidence in a country's financial system.

In addition to these considerations, which are applicable to all countries, the fact that Spain was undergoing a political transition when the banking crisis erupted made the choice clear-cut. There was no other remedy than to find the required resources and to establish the appropriate mechanisms to avoid a general collapse of the Spanish banking system.

Thus, when the first symptoms of the banking crisis were observed in late 1977, a number of measures were adopted which made it possible to deal with the initial banks experiencing difficulties. However, it was not until 1980 that the guarantee fund for bank deposits, which became the basic instrument for coping with the banking crisis, was established in its present form.

4   Initial Approaches to Dealing with the Banking Crisis

Before describing the Deposit Guarantee Fund in detail, it may be instructive to discuss the trial and error period during which the Spanish authorities experimented with a series of alternative approaches before adopting the current model to deal with the crisis.

In 1977, the Bank of Spain relied on a small team of examiners to carry out its supervisory duties.

Their work was largely focused on checking regulatory compliance. This is normal in a system that for several decades had not experienced any serious problems with respect to financial soundness. Even so the Bank of Spain had already identified a significant number of banks in 1977 which were to pose serious problems in the ensuing years. However, the combination of its inexperience in dealing with such a new situation and the lack of accuracy in identifying bank losses made it difficult for the Bank of Spain to come up rapidly with a good formula to deal with the problem. Generally, the banks themselves classed their insolvency problems as simple, temporary liquidity difficulties, which the Bank of Spain as lender of last resort dealt with using its rediscount facility.

However, in view of the weaknesses in their discounted portfolios, the Bank of Spain decided to use this approach selectively, that is, only for those banks whose management it could trust. Thus, in 1978, the Bank of Spain set up a private management company called Corporación Bancaria owned 50/50 with the private banks to administer those banks with chronic liquidity problems. In order for Corporación Bancaria to gain ownership and management rights, the Bank of Spain required that the new liquidity facility be made available only to those banks (some of which were in fact insolvent) that had sold a controlling interest to the new institution for 1 peseta. Once Corporación Bancaria became the principal owner of a bank, it also took over its management. In financial circles, it came to be known as the 'Bank Hospital', a name that would later be inherited by the Deposit Guarantee Fund which eventually succeeded Corporación Bancaria.

While this approach solved liquidity problems, it did not address the fundamental underlying problem of restoring the banks' capital base. The longer this situation lasted, the more serious it became. Without the power to deal with the problem of capital, Corporación Bancaria was limited in its ability to disclose the true state of banks' financial condition to the common shareholders, since in practice, it proved impossible to declare a bank failure publicly without either closing the institution immediately, rebuilding capital, or offering some prospect of future normalization.

5   The Deposit Guarantee Fund

In 1980, almost three years after the crisis began, the Spanish authorities established an institution known as the Deposit Guarantee Fund for banking institutions (the Fund). It played a leading and effective role in resolving the majority of bank problems in Spain. The Fund combines the management functions carried out by Corporación Bancaria with the deposit guarantee function. It is legally able to assume bank ownership and has the financial resources to reconstruct the capital of problem banks. At the same time, procedures were established to promote third-party purchase of problem banks as an ultimate solution. (Following the creation of the Fund for commercial banks, the Deposit Guarantee Fund for savings banks and the guarantee fund for credit unions were set up, ensuring since 1982 that all private institutions in the Spanish financial system are covered by a similar guarantee arrangement.)

After 1980, the rehabilitation of the Spanish banking system was accomplished through the mechanisms set up by these Funds. Nevertheless, there was one important exception—the Rumasa Group, which comprised 20 banks and 300 enterprises. Because of its special characteristics, the Spanish authorities decided to deal with the Group not through the Fund, but by temporary nationalization. This special case will be described briefly, later on, as an illustration of a different approach to bank restructuring.

6   Main Features of the Fund

To simplify, I shall refer basically to the Fund for banks, which, owing to the volume of its operations and intensity of its activities, is the most representative prototype.

The Fund was created by law in March 1980, as a public body governed by the rules of private law. The objective of the Fund is to protect depositors in two ways:

1. by ensuring small depositors will be made whole in the event an institution is closed; and
2. alternatively, by ensuring the continued survival of a bank though whatever actions are necessary to restore its solvency and return it to normal operations. While the Bank of Spain retains the 'lender of last resort' function, the Fund serves as the mandatory channel through which bank insolvency problems are tackled.

Assessments to the Fund are paid in equal shares by the private banking community and by the Bank of Spain. The Fund's member banks make annual contributions, which are considered an expenditure item in their income statement. The size of these contributions is calculated as a proportion (ranging between 1 and 3 per thousand) of each bank's deposit liabilities. The current rate is 2.5 per thousand of deposits. The Bank of Spain makes an annual contribution equal to the total contributions of all the banks. Because the Fund was established in the midst of the crisis and the financial resources from the assessment system proved insufficient, the Bank of Spain was empowered by law to make long-term loans at the rediscount rate to the Fund, with no limit.

The Fund is governed by an eight-member Board of Directors. Four of its members are bankers of acknowledged standing (appointed by the Ministry of Economy upon proposal by the Bank of Spain), who serve in their individual capacity and not as representatives of their banks. The remaining four are Directors of the Bank of Spain. The Board is chaired by a representative of the Bank of Spain, who casts the deciding vote in the event of a tie. The executive director of the Fund carries the title of Secretary General and manages a staff (120 persons at its peak down to 40 currently) who perform the tasks entrusted to the institution.

To ensure the continuity of bank operations and purchase arrangements, the Fund is empowered to act on a broad scale and may extend credit to its bank members, purchase all types of assets (shares, loans, real estate, etc.), provide guarantees, assume losses and subscribe capital of banks and non-banking institutions. In the event that an institution is liquidated, the Fund guarantees the equivalent of $15,000 for each depositor and creditors' rights revert to the Fund in all cases. With a view to restoring the capital of a problem bank, the Fund may first request a bank to ask its shareholders to participate in a capital increase. However, if this is not fully subscribed by the shareholders, the Fund is empowered to subscribe the capital increase directly. The Fund also has the power to require its members to submit their financial statements to external auditors as often and with as much detail as necessary. Failure by a member institution to comply with the obligations arising from any of the foregoing points constitutes sufficient grounds for the Fund to expel the member bank.

Once the fund has assumed the control of an institution, it can provide a financial assistance package to clean up the bank and organize its subsequent takeover by other shareholders, as a final step in the rehabilitation process. To do this, the Fund must put the bank up for sale to institutions which have the necessary qualifications and solvency to ensure the normal operation of the bank in the future. The offer must be sufficiently publicized, competitive and occur within one year following the date on which the Fund took over ownership of the bank.

7   Operation of the Fund

For illustration purposes, it may be useful to give a description of how the Fund might handle a typical case where external audits, or examination by the Bank of Spain, identify a shortage of capital in a bank.

If the shortage is slight, it is sufficient for the bank to adjust its accounts and increase its capital to the extent necessary.

If there is a serious shortage of capital and the shareholders are not able or willing to increase it, then the course of action is more complex. In fact,

Spanish law, other than through bankruptcy procedures, does not provide either for the temporary suspension of rights derived from share ownership or for the administration of an entity to pass to a public institution such as the Fund. In view of this legal constraint, the Fund must have access to bank ownership and continue to manage the bank as a going concern, until such time as its capital has been sold to third parties.

The Fund has two alternative routes to ownership: it can purchase a controlling interest from the previous owners at the symbolic price of one peseta per share if agreement can be reached, or else, it can subscribe a capital increase, authorized by the governing bodies of the bank concerned. To ensure that the previous owners sell at a symbolic price or authorize the capital increase, the Fund informs the bank facing insolvency that, if its shareholders cannot reconstitute its capital, the bank's membership in the Fund will be cancelled with due publicity. In addition, the Bank of Spain can condition its role as lender of last resort on the outcome of either of the decisions. Both arguments carry great weight.

Special mention should be made of the mechanism applied in Spain and known financial circles as an 'accordion operation' which consists of a simultaneous reduction and increase in capital. Such an operation has a double objective: to write off potential bank losses and to penalize previous shareholders by diluting or virtually writing off their participation in ownership. In this way, the central government, the banking system and the shareholders together form a cost-sharing triangle. The 'accordion' system involves an operation in which a bank experiencing difficulties writes off all its reserves and all or part of its share capital, depending on the magnitudes of existing bank losses. This operation is simultaneously followed by a capital increase for the amount required to establish capital and reserve levels commensurate with the bank's size. The Bank of Spain usually orders the bank to make this increase and, lacking other subscribers, the Fund subscribes it. This is the most frequent method used by the Fund to achieve majority ownership of the bank.

This now leaves the Fund as the principal owner of the bank. The Fund then removes the current senior management and appoints a new management team, whose efforts will be primarily focused on the following aspects: keeping the bank running, verification of accounts, restructuring and sale of the majority interest owned by the Fund. In particular, it must determine the bank's true financial situation, which almost always proves to be more serious than had first been perceived in the course of routine analysis, audit and examination procedures. It must also undertake restructuring measures, often of a surgical nature, in the bank's major problem areas, for example, securing and collection of loans, liquidation of fixed assets, reduction in financial costs and cuts in staff and general overheads. Next, it is tasked with the design of a financial assistance package

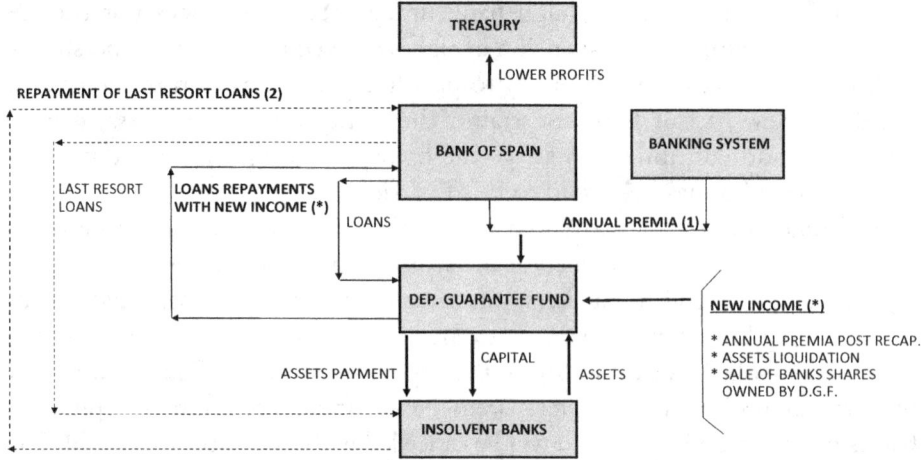

Fig. 2.2 Spain: financial restructuring

to be provided by the Fund, which mainly consists of the purchase of assets and long-term loans to restore the bank's solvency and profitability. This package is the basis on which the bank is ultimately offered to sale.

These tasks are supposed to be carried out within 12 months, since legislation requires that once the Fund has owned the bank for one year, it must put up its shares for sale. According to its own internal rules, the Fund coordinates a selective bidding procedure with adequate publicity, to sell to the highest bidder among the interested solvent banking institutions. Once a bank is awarded to a buyer, normally a much larger bank, the Fund provides the financial assistance noted previously, usually the purchase of non-productive and/or doubtful assets at book value. This brings us to the final stage in the sequence of the Fund's activities: the liquidation of assets and their temporary management until liquidation. (Figure 2.2 shows the institutions, operations and flows used for financial restructuring of banks by the Fund.)

8   The Rumasa Case

The Rumasa, S.A. holding company was a special case in the history of the Spanish banking crisis. The group included over 300 companies, including 20 banks, and over 200 industrial and service firms. Altogether, the holding company employed more than 50,000 people, including 11,000 in the banking sector. Sixty percent of total loans were concentrated heavily within its own group (a large part of which were hidden).

Given the scope of the problems, the Fund approach posed serious difficulties. First, the financial resources needed to rehabilitate Rumasa would have exceeded the Fund's financial capacity. Second, had the Fund become involved, it would have immediately faced another dilemma—either to interrupt the financing of the 200 companies, which would have resulted in their liquidation, or else to perpetuate and aggravate the concentration of risks in companies that were in many cases insolvent. Under these circumstances, the government promulgated an ad hoc emergency law nationalizing Rumasa S.A. The same law simultaneously established a mechanism to appraise the value of shares held in Rumasa, and it also stated the government's intention to return the group to private hands.

Once the group was nationalized, the government turned over the management of its 20 banks to the Fund, and appointed different administrators for the holding company and remaining businesses. One year later, the reprivatization process of all the group companies began. The banks were sold in a block to the seven largest Spanish banks, which subsequently divided them among themselves.

The rehabilitation process of the Rumasa banks also involved the following financial manoeuvring. The Spanish Government issued public debt bonds for the amount of Ptas. 400 billion at 9.5% interest per annum repayable over 12 years. The public debt issue was subscribed by the 12 largest Spanish banks in proportion to their customers' deposits. The Government used the Ptas. 400 billion from the public debt issue to make an interest-free loan to Rumasa, S.A., which in turn used the money from the loan to repay its debts and those of other member companies to the group's own banks. Using the proceeds from the loan repayments and other assessments, the Rumasa Group Banks made interbank deposits in the 12 major banks for an amount equal to the amount of public debt bonds subscribed by each bank and with identical maturity, but bearing interest at a rate of 13.5% per annum.

From the date of their expropriation to the date of their sale, the Bank of Spain also lent the Rumasa Group Banks Ptas. 400 billion at 8% per annum to finance their commitments to their creditors and temporarily keep the group's companies in operation until they could be sold or liquidated. This loan was to be amortized over a 12-year period, indirectly using the funds received from the government.

As the public debt issue reached maturity, that is, when the 12 banks pay off the deposits received from the Rumasa banks, the latter repay their loan to the Bank of Spain. In effect, the government was paying the 12 major banks that subscribed the public bond issue.

By means of these operations, the financial position and economic situation of the Rumasa Group Banks remained as follows:

– Regarding capital and reserves, the assets remained solvent by replacing Ptas. 400 billion in bad loans with cash received from the government.
– Economically, for 12 years, although decreasingly, the financial margin of the ailing banks would benefit from the 5.5% differential between the interest rate on Bank of Spain loan to the Rumasa banks (8.0%) and that on the deposits placed in the 12 banks by the latter (13.5%).

The cost of this rehabilitation operation for the government is

– the repayment of the debt issue for the next 12 years, minus the amounts to be recovered from the loan it extended to Rumasa, S.A., which in all likelihood will cover less than 25% of the full amount of the Ptas 400 billion loan.
– The cost to the banking community is the interest rate differential between the cost of the cash deposits it had taken at 13.5% and the proceeds from subscription of the public debt issue, 9.5%, which would decrease over the next 12 years.

As can be seen, the financial restructuring operation was a closed circuit of cash movements, which over the next 12 years will be broken by the redemption of the public debt issue and by the banking sector's payment of the interest rate differential.

9   Results and Lessons Learned

In sum, of the 52 Spanish banks suffering serious financial difficulties, only three small banks were closed. Their depositors were paid off by the government. Another 49 banks, which were financially rehabilitated by the Fund or the state, were sold to other larger solvent banks. In all cases, ownership and management were changed. These 49 banks are all now operating normally either as subsidiaries of larger banks, or have been merged with them.

Financial outlays required during the Fund's first five years of operation have far exceeded the combined annual contributions from the private banking sector and the Bank of Spain. For this reason, the Bank of Spain has had to make large long-term loans to the Fund. The proceeds from the liquidations carried out by the Fund, together with the successive annual assessments to the Fund, should make it possible for the Bank of Spain to be fully reimbursed by 1994.

The costs incurred by the banks and the government amounted to some $10 billion. However, the inflation rate, which was some 25% in 1977, was gradually reduced to 11% in 1984, when the crisis came to an end. Tax reforms and an effective open market operation compensated the monetary flows derived from the banking crisis. The loss, in budgetary terms, was spread over a period of 14 years through the procedure described. Finally, the international banking sector, whose deposits the Bank of Spain offered to cover, never made use of this facility and maintained confidence in the Spanish financial system.

Note

The Spanish banking crisis of the 1980s is now history. The mechanisms that were applied to deal with it were drawn mainly from the American toolkit. This crisis taught the author a number of lessons, which are described in Chap. 1, and after 1987 these lessons came to be used as a kind of handbook by the World Bank for many years, providing a series of rules of thumb to define the conditionality of its loans to a range of countries. It was also the backbone of the international training programmes of the Federal Reserve Board (FED) for a number of years.

Spelled out in the Note to Chap. 1, these lessons remain fresh and applicable in 2019.

3

The Microeconomic Roots
of the Banking Crises

*Bad management is just as important as macroeconomic factors in the origin and
exacerbation of banking crises. And it is easier to control.*
A. de Juan

1   The Roots of Banking Crises: Microeconomic,
Supervisory and Legislative Issues

1. According to one school of thought, all banking crises ultimately have macroeconomic roots and the only thing that matters is the *real economy*. The economists who hold this belief see the financial sector as no more than a sub-product of the real economy. This point of view is shared by many bankers, who seem to believe that their own bad management is never to blame. They are joined by not a few politicians, who find it easier to avoid taking corrective action or restructuring, whether of the industry as a whole or individual banks on a case-by-case basis.

2. This school holds, then, that banks and banking should give no cause for concern when the economy is prospering, and that the industry's health can be taken as read. When an economy is in trouble, however, there should still be no special focus on the financial sector, since there will be little that can actually be done to remedy its woes.

Excerpt from an address delivered to numerous central bankers and experts at the Inter-American Development Bank in Washington in 1994. Among those present were Paul Volcker (former Governor of the FED) and Luis Angel Rojo (Governor of the Bank of Spain at that time).

© The Author(s) 2019
A. de Juan, *From Good to Bad Bankers*,
https://doi.org/10.1007/978-3-030-11551-7_3

3. Nevertheless, international experience tells us that good banks still operate successfully in the midst of recession, and that some banks fail even in boom times. What is the key to this apparent contradiction? It is management. Good management can help an institution weather any macroeconomic storm, while bad management can sink a bank even when conditions are balmy.

4. Let me recall my time at the head of the Bank of Spain's Inspection Department during the Spanish depression and banking crisis of the 1980s. Every time a bank was diagnosed as insolvent and a decision was sought from the Bank of Spain's Board on how to address the problem, the directors would ask about the reasons for the institution's failure and my answer was always the same—bad management.

5. We might also mention the survey of bank insolvencies published in 1988 by the US Office of the Comptroller of the Currency. This study assessed contributing factors in the failure of national banks based on an analysis of institutions that went under in the period 1979–1987. The conclusion reached was that most bank failures were caused by the poor quality of assets and the accompanying erosion of the victims' equity. However, it was also found that bad management at the banks affected, and not the general economic climate, was the key factor to blame for poor asset quality. According to the survey, banks can continue to operate as viable institutions in spite of economic ups and downs provided they establish and uphold sound policies, systems and internal controls.

So, banking problems and bank failures are in fact almost never solely due to conditions of economic depression.

6. Be this as it may, it would be very difficult to establish in general terms the proportions in which it is wider economic conditions or bad management that trigger banking crises. This can only be done by examining each country and bank individually. It could, however, be said that macroeconomic variables outweigh microeconomic factors in 'systemic' crises, while the latter are more important in isolated bank failures. In any event, 'systemic' crises generally involve more severe individual difficulties for some banks because they are badly run. These crises are often ignored, however, or are lumped in with the rest. We may conclude, then, that macroeconomic factors are usually accompanied by microeconomic ills in situations of both systemic and individual crises.

7. Though it has been said that regulation can sometimes magnify the incentives to indulge in risky management practices, this author believes that poor prudential regulation and lax supervision are among the key reasons for bank failure, because the absence of strict controls and appropriate corrective measures creates a breeding ground for bad management.

8. Bad management, with all of its implications for a bank's financial health, can take root in many different circumstances, but two typical situations stand out.

8.1. There is the moment when a new banker arrives on the scene, either by creating a fledgling bank from scratch or by acquiring an existing institution. Prevailing policies, systems and practices may prove inadequate at such times, and sometimes the funds used by the aspiring banker for his venture, whether it takes the form of a new institution or an acquisition, are at least guaranteed, and maybe even provided, by the bank itself.

8.2. Then there is the case of veteran bankers who continue at the helm of existing banks but cannot keep up with changes in fast-developing markets. Veteran bankers too can lead their banks downhill when problems begin to emerge but are not recognized in the institution's accounts. In fact, it is universally the case that unrecognized problems cannot be corrected, because they 'don't exist' either in the accounts or in the eyes of the general public. Examples of banks with seriously impaired assets seeking to prevent their problems from emerging and to avoid the corrective attentions of the national supervisory authorities are to be found almost everywhere.

9. The typical characteristics of bad management are overextension, breakneck growth and weak lending policies, internal controls and planning procedures. Any one of these factors, or any combination of them, can cause operating losses, erode capital and eventually wreck an institution.

10. Overextension may be defined as 'doing too much', and of course a banker can 'do too much' in different ways, as we shall see.

10.1. A bank can become overextended when it lends too much in proportion to its equity or deposit base. In the first case, the bank is relatively decapitalized and its 'cushion' against losses (i.e. its equity) may prove insufficient if its loan book suffers significant impairment. A bank can also lend too much in proportion to its deposit base. It will then need to seek additional funding in the interbank market, sometimes to such an extent that its financial balance and stability may be affected by the volatility of borrowings and the narrowing of financial margins.

10.2. The expression 'overextension' may also be used in geographical terms. Banks sometimes decide to set up in new countries without understanding very clearly why they are doing so or assuring adequate control of their overseas businesses. It may be that they are too keen to follow the trend, which is actually a widespread vice among bankers. 'If everybody is internationalizing, why shouldn't I?' This author personally knows of a Spanish bank which decided at a given moment to pursue an aggressive international policy even though the key directors of its international operations hardly spoke foreign languages and were not prepared to make more than occasional visits to the institution's offices abroad.

10.3. Another manifestation of overextension is unbridled product diversification. Faced with strict international capital adequacy rules, most banks seek to diversify their products to boost their income from fees and commissions. There is of course nothing wrong with this strategy, but some banks diversify to excess in the hope that their new source of income may eventually surpass the returns generated on their loan books. This is a very risky policy unless a bank has the expertise to manage new products and its control systems are strong and sophisticated enough to cope. The examples of derivatives products in general spring immediately to mind. The watchword here must be, 'Don't do what you don't understand well or cannot properly control.'

11. Headlong and crudely aggressive growth is another typical cause of problems that can eventually lead to bank failure. The pursuit of growth for growth's sake is a syndrome that affects many bankers. All bankers dream of their becoming the biggest bank and of leading the pack in their home country, even where they run the risk of undermining their institution's own profits or stability. The ambition to win major customers and to secure a place at the top table can often drive bankers into a mad dash for growth. Once again, this can be a very risky. In the first place, a rapidly expanding bank will have to pay high rates of interest to grow its funding apace, adversely affecting its financial margins. Furthermore, this policy can lead a bank to become financially overextended so that it depends too heavily on interbank borrowing with all of its concomitant hazards. Also, when the goal is to grow fast, the pursuit of opportunities to make new loans can become a matter of life or death. In these circumstances, loan selection criteria tend to slip, resulting in a deterioration in the quality of the loan book.

12. Poor credit policy is another key factor in banking crises. The primary function of any sound bank is to place the savings it attracts in the market in such a way as to assure a satisfactory return and the recovery of loans. Hence, bankers must never forget that the funds they loan out belong to other people and not to themselves, and these savings must eventually be returned. Where banks fail to observe this principle, they inevitably fall prey to illiquidity and insolvency. That is why bad lending practices are so often at the heart of banking crises. Such bad practice includes risk concentration, irresponsible lending to related parties, mismatches between the terms of loans and the liabilities used to fund them, interest and exchange rate risks, and weak recovery practices.

13. The concentration of risks is a typical cause of bank failure. Concentration in certain borrowers or groups of borrowers or in segments of the economy or geographic regions of a country runs counter to the principle of risk diversification, which is key to sound banking. This high risk is easily explained—default

by a small group of borrowers or crisis in a given segment of the market can imperil the lender's position. The strategies and practices concerned are always risky when the banker applies them voluntarily based on erroneous assessments of credit quality, but they are all the more so when the borrower is linked to the bank or the banker, as we shall see below.

Risk concentration may also be an involuntary process, however, when a significant part of originally good quality loans granted by a bank are later frozen and the institution finds itself constrained to continue lending to bad borrowers in the hope of finding a way out. In such cases, a bank will also renew the loans granted, refinancing and capitalizing the interest due. If it did not, the borrowers would default and both their difficulties and those of the bank itself would become public knowledge. This is something that most bankers would do anything to avoid. Where the malaise spreads to other banks, the economy as a whole may suffer.

14. Banks sometimes also engage in speculation. This may involve lending to high-risk borrowers in the hope of obtaining a bigger return. While contractual interest rates may reflect this strategy, it is actually much less likely to be borne out in terms of the actual interest paid, because the kind of borrowers who are willing to accept high interest rates on paper are generally the very ones who will eventually default on their obligations. High interest rates also skew the client selection process. Speculation can also involve lending and investment in real estate and the stock market, especially at times of high inflation, when borrowers and bankers alike hope to disinvest quickly with significant gains. Things almost never turn out quite like that, however. Anti-inflationary policies cause stagnation and markets fall, and instead of recovering past losses a bank is only too likely to see its assets locked in as further losses pile up.

15. In this speculative, high-risk phase, a bank will most likely already have serious liquidity problems, and it will therefore seek fresh funds in the form of deposits, credits or interbank loans at any cost. Cash may also be needed to meet transformation costs. When a bank pays high interest rates for such funds, it is because it hopes to maintain its own margin by passing on the cost to borrowers, which often proves counterproductive.

16. By this point, the market will probably have noticed a bank's difficulties and investors may begin to sell their shares. Those enjoying inside information about a bank's condition may also sometimes dump shares onto the market to recover their investment before it is too late. The resulting fall in the share price marks the beginning of the process of deterioration. To prevent this, and to shore up the value of their own personal holdings, bankers may have the institution buy its own shares in the market or from themselves,

either directly or via affiliates or straw companies financed by the bank itself. This treasury stock not only distorts the market at the expense of minority shareholders, but also results in additional losses and further erodes equity, even if this effect is concealed.

17. This process ends in illiquidity. It is only then that the ineffective supervisor will discover the situation of insolvency previously existing behind the veil of fictitious accounting. The problem here is that a problem bank may already have been insolvent for quite some while before its actual condition is revealed, and in this time its problems will only have grown, making them much costlier to resolve in the end. Except when illiquidity is widespread throughout the system as a result of macroeconomic conditions, it could be said that any lasting situation of illiquidity found in a bank points to underlying insolvency, which may have remained concealed for a significant period.

18. Last but not least, fraud is also at the root of some banking failures. In the first place, cosmetic accounting practices can easily cross the line into outright fraud, especially in an industry like banking that is based on public trust. Numerous other fraudulent practices exist, however, the commonest being bogus lending by the bank to the banker, where the transaction is arranged in such a way that balances will never be repaid. The commonest scams of this kind are to grant loans via straw companies, to waive the requirement for collateral or to lift guarantees before the foreclosure term.

19. Related-party loans are another common cause of banking crises, and they often result in a concentration of lending. Therefore, they are exposed to all of the concentration risks described above, as well as the other hazards mentioned in this section. Related-party loans may involve lending to affiliates of the bank, of the banker, or of the banker's friends and associates.

19.1. It is quite typical for universal and development banks to grant loans to their investee companies where the terms of their banking licences allow them to own shares in non-financial firms. This was the case with the majority of the banks that went under in the Spanish banking crisis of the 1980s. There is in fact nothing wrong with this practice in principle, provided the bank operates at arm's length under normal market conditions. The problem arises when the transactions in question involve overly generous terms or amounts; when the availability of related-party credit makes the managers of an affiliate lazy because their company's liquidity is assured; and when the loans made muddy information flows between the borrower and the bank. The trouble in the latter case is that banks are generally represented by their own senior executives in the affiliated borrower, who paradoxically hinder effective information gathering by the parent so that non-performing loans are rarely classified as such. Hence, no provisions are made and recovery procedures are not set in motion. Loans of this kind are especially risky in publicly owned institutions, if they cloud short-and long-term social objectives or if the banks themselves come under political pressure to continue lending to insolvent borrowers or to refrain from seeking recovery of the loans due.

19.2. Lending to affiliates by bankers or their friends and associates treads a fine line with fraud, and may cross it. After all, this practice means using management power and the bank's (i.e. other people's) money for the benefit of the banker himself. Bad faith and negligence are likely from the outset in such transactions, and may even be part of the banker's purpose in granting the loan.

19.3. Mismatch or asymmetry of repayment terms is another source of banking problems due to the liquidity risk it implies. Such mismatches may be the result of a deliberate strategy on the part of the banker, or they may arise when initially sound loans made under reasonable repayment terms are frozen and maturities are extended due to default or the agreement of a new repayment schedule. It is of course true that the transformation of terms lies at the heart of the banking business, but it has its limits. It is also true that mismatches are more likely to cause liquidity problems when they are due to slow asset churn (relative asset volatility), and they can trigger failures. Let us not forget, meanwhile, that illiquidity caused by asset churn problems is closely linked to insolvency, insofar as non-performing assets tend to display very slow turnover rates. Be this as it may, it is likely that any successes achieved by a bank in resolving its liquidity problems will be accompanied by an increase in the cost of the funds it needs to continue its business and, therefore, a diminution in profits. Some banks, lacking the necessary expertise to manage the timing of their operations, embark upon a policy of growth based on the transformation of funds borrowed in the overnight market into loans with much longer terms. This policy brings them straight to the brink of illiquidity, forcing them to take painful measures to speed up the churn in their loan books and shrink their balance sheets.

19.4. Nemesis often appears in the guise of interest rate risk. In statistical terms, this risk does not usually trigger crises in the same way as insolvency, but it is frequently the cause of shrinking profits. It may take various forms. Problems most commonly arise when interest rates are affected by sharp fluctuations (especially in times of deregulation), when the total cost of deposits rises steeply, and when all or a significant part of loans are made at fixed rates of interest. Another situation of risk is found where interest rates fall sharply and banks holding large portfolios of public debt see the value of their investments shrink significantly in the market.

19.5. Exchange rate risk also exists in various forms. There is the case of foreign currency loans made to countries whose reserves become exhausted, and which then default on their payment obligations for ever, or at least for very long periods. In times of devaluation, meanwhile, borrowers may default if their businesses cannot generate the necessary foreign currency, or if the exchange rate makes repayment in local currency prohibitively expensive. Another form of exchange rate risk appears when a bank borrows in foreign currency which it then changes into local currency to lend at a much higher interest rate. In the short term, this generates a profit, but it comes with a serious exchange rate risk attached—the borrower can repay the loan in local currency, but any devaluation will make it much costlier for the bank to amortize its own foreign currency debt.

19.6. Weak recovery procedures are commonly found in developing nations. When major borrowers run into difficulties with the repayment of loans, they often seek tacit agreements with their banks to avoid formal bankruptcy, leading to a 'can't pay/won't collect' scenario in which the debtor defaults but the lender refrains from enforcement. Weak recovery procedures are also often associated with related-party loans and other fraudulent practices where the banker makes no effort to collect on the debts due. Moreover, legislation governing the enforcement of loans and insolvency, not to mention the antiquated legal procedures still existing in many countries, mean that recovery through the courts can be a long and wearisome process. In this context, it might be asked whether the weakness of loan recovery in Latin America is due to ineffective bankruptcy laws or to bad management. Though it has not been statistically shown to be the case, it seems that bad management is largely to blame, not only at the moment of recovery but also when the loans concerned are first made. The problem, then, is that a weak lending policy implies that the largest borrowers are likely to have limited capacity to repay their loans, regardless of how effective actual enforcement and bankruptcy processes may be. The result is lax recovery procedures, which are sometimes further stymied by tacit complicity between borrowers and their banks.

20. The failure of internal controls is also sometimes to blame for banking crises. Such failures have always existed, of course, but the appearance of derivatives and hybrid products now requires ever more sophisticated techniques and technologies. A lack of internal control can be fatal. Weak internal controls may be due to either or both of the following:

1. Poor lending decisions and ineffective risk monitoring systems.
2. Dysfunctional information systems that provide insufficient and/or irrelevant data for proper, timely analysis.

21. Finally, there is the matter of bad planning. Business planning is a sophisticated matter and, though it may not always assure the attainment of goals, it certainly helps firms stay on track and avoid losing their way. If we treat planning as mindset rather than viewing it in terms of process and techniques, it could be said that bankers all too often believe that 'nothing too serious ever happens', and they therefore fail to adapt to change, whether in terms of strategy, products, technology or the makeup of their own management team. Attitudes of this kind will not cause any immediate trouble, but they may lead a bank into a slow decline, ending with its eventual demise, although it is actually more likely to be bought out by new investors or merged with a stronger institution than actually wound up. This is the typical case of banks whose senior managers have grown old and become too set in their ways.

22. If prudential legislation and regulation are strong enough to reign in the practices described above, and if supervisory mechanisms are effective enough to assure compliance and the enforcement of effective corrective measures, then problems can probably be nipped in the bud, or at least identified early on. If so, banking crises will become less frequent and damaging. On this assumption, any recapitalization that might be needed could be effected before the erosion of a significant part of a problem bank's capital, and any managers shown to be incompetent should be given short shrift, whatever their seniority. The problem is that legislation is not always effective, while bankers may be loath to take corrective action and oversight is all too often toothless. In these circumstances, problems can mushroom while bankers dedicate their efforts to creative accounting and cosmetic measures.

Note

The features of the model described in Chap. 1 and the lessons learned are merely sketched out there for the sake of simplicity.

In this light, I have expanded some of the concepts outlined in Chap. 1, as well as describing other common management and supervisory shortcomings.

4

'False Friends' and Banking Reform

However large the arsenal of financial reforms and regulations may appear, it will
all prove useless, and maybe even counterproductive, if they only go half way.
A. de Juan

1   'Good Friends' and Banking Reform

1. The problems discussed here refer primarily to banking systems in transition economies, but they apply equally to other economies where banking reform has been undertaken. We shall begin by sketching out the progress made in transition economies in recent years and will then go on to warn about the dangers of 'paper reforms' and doing things half way. These pitfalls are what is here meant by the expression 'false friends'.

2. The progress achieved in transition economies is outlined below:

2.1. Formerly monolithic banks have been broken up to foster *competition*. Meanwhile, new banking licenses have also been issued and financial markets deregulated.

2.2. *New banking laws, accounting systems and prudential regulations* have been enacted to address basic matters like profit, capital and provisions for potential losses.

2.3. *New supervisory institutions* have been created and existing arrangements have been tightened up, seeking to cut down on bureaucracy and focus on the quality of the financial system as a whole and on individual banks.

Address given at the Annual Meeting of the European Bank for Reconstruction and Development held in London in April 1995.

2.4. Some countries have set up *deposit guarantee schemes* to protect depositors in the event of bank failures.

2.5. Some have launched *bank restructuring* processes in response to widespread insolvency. These initiatives are sometimes accompanied by measures to encourage *mergers* as a means of changing the ownership and weeding out the management of weaker institutions, or in order to reverse the proliferation of new banks and create larger organizations.

2.6. *Privatization* of former state-owned banks has begun in some countries, as a means to enhance competition, improve management quality and foster market control mechanisms.

2.7. Numerous countries have fostered in-house and external *training* as a means of strengthening the management of local banks, sometimes with the assistance of multinational institutions.

3. All of these efforts deserve our recognition and support, and all of them address issues that must be tackled to build sound banking systems. However, it is too early yet for complacency, and still less for the indulgence of self-congratulation. Reform in the context of transition economies is bound to be a drawn-out process, and there is still a long hard road ahead.

4. This chapter sounds a cautionary note based on the author's experience in a number of countries, both developing and developed, in the hope that these *warnings* will prove useful to governments and banks alike as they walk the path of reform.

5. Insolvency is widespread in transition economies, and not only there, affecting both carve-out banks spun off from formerly monolithic institutions and newly licensed banks, many of which are still very green and have not yet put down firm roots. Hence, these remarks are made from the standpoint of insolvency, and not all of them will be universally applicable. The author has two main reasons for advising caution. In the first place, progress is very uneven from country to country, although considerable headway has clearly been made overall; and in the second, progress may vary considerably from one area of reform to another even in the same country.

6. The warnings presented here are not intended to form an exhaustive list, but to highlight the pitfalls or 'false friends' that may be found in the context of finance industry reform. They refer, then, to concepts and policies which may have their own merits but can also prove useless, and even counterproductive, in isolation or when they clash with other essential measures, or if they are only half-heartedly applied. Specifically, the 'false friends' introduced here reside in the areas of regulation, supervision, restructuring, privatization and institution building.

7. In the area of regulation, we shall discuss five concepts, to wit, market access, minimum capital requirements, assets classification, accounting systems and (the absence of) adequate supervision.

7.1. Boosting competition by opening up the market to new banks and bankers is to be applauded. However, the *market access policies* implemented in some countries have been overly lax, with the result that entrepreneurs and firms have flocked to set up new banks merely as a means of getting their hands on cash funds. In other words, banks are too often created with minimal capital (sometimes actually borrowed by the new banks' shareholders) and are then used to take deposits from the public, which are then loaned out primarily to undertakings and ventures owned by the institution's shareholders. This is a sure recipe for failure. Moreover, governments are often loth to address the problems of such entities when they run into difficulties, so that the market ends up crowded with 'zombie banks', undermining competition and distorting the efficient allocation of resources. The entry of new banks is therefore a highly positive development, but it may prove a 'false friend' if they do not meet certain minimum standards for starting capital, which must be high and originate from clearly identified sources, and for the integrity and expertise of the bankers themselves. In addition, it is essential to ensure a proper match between liberal market access and tough market exit policies, which should prioritize the closure and liquidation of insolvent banks.

It has been argued that criticism of liberal market access policies of access is often used to keep competitors out and protect incumbents. This may be so, but the situation outlined above is likely to materialize only where policies are overly lax. Another school of thought holds, meanwhile, that the starting capital required to found a bank should not be set too high so as to shut out potentially sound candidates capable of operating smaller institutions serving local clients. In such cases, the starting capital required for the formation of a new bank could be lowered, but the range of its business should also be restricted accordingly. For example, it could be excluded from the payments system and its geographic expansion could be limited unless and until capital is increased.

7.2. Adequate *capital* is a must. Most governments and banks now accept the Basel Committee guidelines, which require banks to hold minimum capital equal to 8% of risk-weighted assets. This goes some way to ensuring that banks are healthy and financially sound, and it also sets a standard, placing domestic and international competitors on an equal footing. The problem is that governments and banks will sometimes proudly proclaim that they have a capital ratio of 8%, 10% or even 11%, while paying scant attention to the quality of their assets. When a bank claims to have a capital adequacy ratio of 10%, for instance, but also has undisclosed losses equal to 30% of its assets, its true capital ratio will be −20%. Capital adequacy rules are indeed crucial, but they are clearly a 'false friend' unless accompanied by sound asset classification standards and mandatory provisioning rules.

7.3. 'Well', a government might retort, '[w]e have a *good asset classification and provisioning system*, which is in line with international standards and is based on payment performance, so that any overdue loans must be reclassified and provided for'. This is as it should be, but if loans are not also classified according to the borrower's repayment capacity (which defines the risk of default) irrespective of whether the loan is or is not overdue, the regulations may once again turn out to be a 'false friend'. Why? Because a bank that is in difficulties will tend to avoid disclosing its losses whether to the supervisor or to the public. Banks holding large non-performing loans that they do not expect to recover will often roll them over when they approach maturity, often more or less indefinitely, in order to avoid the recognition of impairments in their accounts, which could reveal not only default by the borrowers concerned, but potentially also the bank's own insolvency. Experience tells us that the worst loans, those that could drive a bank to the wall, are almost always classified as current and not as overdue. Asset classification regulations may therefore also be considered a 'false friend', where it is left up to the banks themselves to make the necessary allowances rather than requiring mandatory provisions. The same is true where institutions are permitted to recognize income in respect of interest capitalized on rollovers. Such regulations allow banks to appear sound and profitable, using regulatory compliance to cloak insolvency and losses.

7.4. One of the prerequisites for the proper assessment of solvency and classification of assets is a *sound reporting system*. Without a meaningful application of modern accounting standards, financial reporting may become merely an exercise in 'garbage in garbage out' as the computer scientists like to say, making a proper diagnosis of an institution's situation all but impossible not only for the supervisor, but also for bankers themselves. As a consequence, most developing countries have worked hard to establish proper reporting systems. However, a financial reporting system may become a 'false friend' if it fails to include *rules for the consolidation of financial subsidiaries and conglomerates* to ensure the harmonization of items, measurement and internal controls, and to allow regulatory oversight of the consolidated group as a whole. Let us not forget that financial subsidiaries, particularly those operating abroad or off-shore, are favourite places to stash problem assets off the books and out of the supervisor's sight.

7.5. Let us imagine a country that has *made good laws and implemented sound prudential regulations*. This is a great achievement, but if there are no strong supervisory mechanisms to verify the quality of financial institutions and enforce compliance, even this excellent legislative framework will prove a false friend, because the rules will not be applied in a context of insolvency, and so they will gradually be discredited. Good laws and prudential regulations are thus a necessary but not a sufficient condition for the proper functioning of a financial system. They must be supplemented by an adequate supervisory system involving analysis, verification and the application of vigorous corrective measures where needed.

8. This section identifies some 'false friends' found in the area of bank supervision:

8.1. Central banks themselves can become 'false friends' when they also play the role of banking supervisor. Two institutional supervisory systems coexist in the West, depending on whether oversight is entrusted to the central bank or to a separate, independent authority. It is unclear which of these systems is best, but is apparent that oversight can easily become diluted in some transition economies when supervisory functions are handled by the central bank. All of the central banks in the Soviet-style planned economies were at some point *gosbanks* (i.e. state banks that took care of everything, including retail and development banking). However, their role did not involve anything like what we might regard as banking supervision from a commercial standpoint. To some, supervision still means bureaucratic control, statistical research on directed lending to industry and other such tasks intended to assist with economic planning and prevent fraud in the system. In other economies, meanwhile, central bank supervision was entirely secondary to monetary policy. In either case, the option of an independent authority deserves serious consideration, because the new supervisor will have no reason to avoid taking action, in contrast to some central banks, which are adept at finding excuses to shirk their supervisory responsibilities.

8.2. Let us imagine a country that has established a *supervisory mechanism*, which is certainly a major asset for its financial system. Suppose, however, that this mechanism consists only of off-site controls based on the examination of reports filed by the banks themselves. In a context of widespread insolvency, bankers will tend not to disclose their problems and their reports will be largely meaningless. Let us then imagine an alternative scenario in which off-site supervision is accompanied by on-site inspection mechanisms. The progress made will be all the greater. If the number of bank examiners is small, however, and if they lack expertise and are poorly paid, then there is a danger that the supervisory mechanism may become a 'false friend' if government is lulled into the belief that it has taken care of the oversight issue, when this is not in fact the case.

8.3. Many countries have now adopted the practice of *external audit*, whether on a voluntary or mandatory basis. Governments in these countries may also claim that their system now operates according to international standards. What happens, however, when auditors do their work in the context of a deficient regulatory framework? What if the essential communication between external auditors and supervision is not permitted or possible? Once again, we may find ourselves facing a 'false friend', because audit reports are too unreliable. Worse still, they may even be brandished in court or in administrative review proceedings as a weapon against a supervisor trying to use its powers of enforcement or impose remedial measures.

8.4. In another scenario, *supervisory and audit mechanisms may be well designed*, but the supervisor's powers of enforcement may be too feeble, or it may lack appropriate mechanisms to deal with bank restructuring. In such cases, any emerging problems that land on the supervisor's desk are unlikely to be satisfactorily resolved, with the result that supervisory mechanisms will become increasingly discredited and eventually entirely debased. Let me introduce you to a new 'false friend'. Supervision is necessary, but it is not sufficient, and it must be backed up by firm remedial action, sanctions and bank resolution mechanisms.

8.5. Last but not least, there may be cases where *supervisory mechanisms are well designed, enforcement powers are strong and resolution mechanisms are in place*, but government lacks the will to address problems in the financial system. This can happen for political or social reasons, for lack of fiscal resources or for other reasons. In these cases, problems are not solved, the system created with such effort is discredited and, even worse, a certain complicity may develop between bankers, auditors and the government, none of whom will be keen to lay bare harsh realities, which would only be costly and unpopular. This situation is typical of countries where bank restructuring has in truth gone only half way, but it has been loudly proclaimed to the markets that the system has entirely and successfully been overhauled. The government then becomes the prisoner of its own message, so that it may be years before it can again take energetic action because the country's banks are supposed to be in a state of rude health. The inevitable outcomes of such paralysis are the spread of cosmetic accounting and creeping insolvency.

9. 'False friends' may also be found in the area of bank restructuring. When insolvency is widespread in a country, the economy suffers in many ways:

- Payments systems become distorted.
- Resources are allocated preferentially to basket-case companies, crowding out promising new enterprises.

- Interest rates soar as bankers seek to offset flagging returns from much of their loan portfolios.
- The government finds itself forced to offer liquidity support and subsidies to insolvent banks.
- Government will initially take a direct hit in the form of losses incurred by state-owned banks, but as problems pile up throughout the system it will eventually have to foot the bill for public and private sector losses alike.

This is why closing or restructuring insolvent banks is the proper response to situations of widespread insolvency. Meanwhile, the choice between closure or restructuring should be based on a comparison of the two measures in terms of direct costs and possible systemic repercussions.

10. If a bank is deeply insolvent but the shareholders will not or cannot inject any fresh capital and the government decides against closure, it should be thoroughly restructured. This will necessarily involve *recapitalization* by government, which may be effected through the mechanism of a capital injection and/or by carving out bad assets to the full extent required to cover all losses and generate positive *cash flows*. However, it is not enough simply to recapitalize an insolvent bank—it is also necessary to achieve a *change of management and ownership*. In this context some of the restructuring policies that go to make up the conventional wisdom deserve serious criticism as 'false friends', given the urgent need to rebuild cash flows and replace former managers and owners.

10.1. *Inflation will eventually wipe out past losses*, but just letting this happen will not prevent the managers of an insolvent bank from going on lending to the bad old borrowers, and even to new but equally bad ones. This is all too often the case, in fact. 'Bad debtors never die', one might say. Where this happens, the quality of the loan portfolio will only deteriorate further and the underlying situation of insolvency will not be resolved, despite the effect of inflation, which will never be enough unless both managers and owners are replaced.

10.2. In practice, *bank mergers* are only a solution to insolvency if both of the banks involved are well capitalized (or recapitalized, if need be) and one of them, at least, has a strong management team with the necessary skills and expertise to integrate the other successfully. Otherwise, the problems existing in the institutions concerned before the merger will only be compounded. Let us not forget that even mergers between well-capitalized, well-run banks inevitably involve a difficult process of mutual adjustment and power struggles, which can affect the merged institution for years to come. The only exception to this rule is when one of the parties to a merger is large and solvent and the other is insolvent and small. In such cases, the losses of the small bank can sometimes be diluted in the larger institution and the issue of power struggles is less likely to arise.

10.3. *Asset revaluations* can sometimes be used to build up fresh reserves. In times of inflation, banks are sometimes authorized to restate their assets at market value and create the equivalent income and reserves without any tax impact. Measures of this kind generally allow banks to increase their equity per books while avoiding the need for any real capital increase in proportion to the inflationary growth recognized in the balance sheet. One might well ask how such asset revaluation mechanisms could improve the situation of a deeply insolvent institution. The answer is that it cannot. Only an injection of actual capital or the replacement of bad assets by good ones can make any real difference.

10.4. When a central bank provides *ongoing liquidity support and refinances bad loans*, it is treating a solvency problem as if it were a liquidity problem. In cases of deep insolvency, only bucketloads of (very cheap) money would allow a bank to generate a high enough yield to write off the legacy of past losses and begin once again to turn a profit. Since this is impossible in practical terms, ongoing liquidity support will do no more than to keep the bank afloat, but the cash provided will probably only be used to cover general and administrative expenses, and losses will continue to pile up. In the end, the liquidity support provided will be lost if and when the bank is closed. If it is restructured, it will once again be necessary to inject new money in the form of capital. In the meantime, ongoing liquidity support offers bad managers a negative incentive by allowing them to perpetuate their failed administration.

10.5. Governments will sometimes grant *medium-term loans to insolvent banks and/or purchase their medium-term bonds*. Recapitalizing insolvent banks in this way can only succeed if the net margin obtained on the new funds over the term of the loans is enough to absorb the whole stock of losses and then generate positive cash flows. This is hardly possible if the loans are too large or costly to provide a sufficient margin, if their terms are too short, and/or if the bank is illiquid and has to allocate a part of the loans obtained to cover immediate cash outflows, including operating costs.

10.6. Governments will sometimes resort to *callable capital or formal undertakings to increase capital* if necessary as a means of recapitalizing one or more insolvent banks where they lack the necessary funds or political will to complete the process immediately. In technical terms, however, the beneficiary institutions are still bankrupt and bleeding capital, and ministers and officials will be only too well aware of the fact. In these circumstances, the government may formally undertake to subscribe the capital increases needed in order to stave off bankruptcy (which would be obligatory as soon as the extent of the problem bank's difficulties were aired) until fresh funds can be earmarked for recapitalization. This may be a perfectly practical approach. However, governments often imagine that they have done enough and have actually completed the process of financial restructuring, when the truth is that this formula does nothing to improve the insolvent bank's cash flows, which remain negative so that the erosion of its equity continues unabated.

10.7. *Simple debt rescheduling* postpones maturity and foreclosure, as well as offering borrowers some relief in terms of liquidity, but it does nothing to improve their solvency unless the lender banks and/or other creditors (suppliers, government, etc.) agree to write down their claims, or the borrowers themselves undertake a serious process of restructuring to redress their financial position. If this does not happen, a lender will not be able to recuperate its own liquidity and solvency (having undertaken to postpone foreclosure and perhaps even to extend fresh loans). This will be the case even where governments allow provisions to be written back when loans are rescheduled on the (optimistic) assumption that the borrower's solvency will have improved. Worse still, some governments require banks to reschedule their loans to all borrowers across the board, establishing long grace periods before repayments start up again. Such bailouts of borrowers do nothing to improve the situation of creditor banks, however, unless they are accompanied by general restructuring on the part of debtors. Where the balance of principal and interest due is written down, the bank must recognize the full amount of the loss in its financial statements, unless it is directly subsidized by government.

10.8. *Recapitalization may prove insufficient* for numerous reasons, chief among them: (a) the volume of capital injected or assets written off is too small to absorb the stock of losses; (b) a sufficient volume of bad assets is carved out, but the price paid by government is less than face value, leaving all or part of the associated losses in the bank; and (c) capital is injected or asset purchases are paid in the form of low-interest government securities, which do not provide a sufficient spread to generate positive cash flows. All three of these situations are common, and they all mean that the bank concerned has not been properly recapitalized.

10.9. Banks are sometimes recapitalized through capital increases or asset purchases paid with *zero coupon bonds*. The interest accruing over the term of these securities is paid cumulatively in its entirety on maturity, covering the book value of the assets purchased. This formula allows government to defer expenditures, but it might also be asked how it helps a problem bank's cash flows, which will remain negative until compound interest is finally paid on the maturity of the bonds, and how it will improve solvency unless the face value of the bonds is enough to cover not only existing losses but also the ongoing losses incurred over their term.

10.10. Those who favour *debt for equity swaps* as a means to instrument financial restructuring measures will often argue that (a) such arrangements improve a problem bank's solvency by exchanging bad loans for equity in distressed borrowers and (b) the bank can then partner the financial restructuring of the borrower, thereby improving the quality of its asset. This is not necessarily so, however. In fact, any assets a bank may hold in relation to a delinquent debtor, whether loans or shares, will be of the same quality and will require the same provisions. As to restructuring by the banks, international experience has shown that bankers are not always or necessarily good entrepreneurs or managers of industrial and service concerns. Furthermore, a banker who holds equity in a borrower company is likely to come under intense pressure to go on making loans, even if the company's situation does not improve or worsens.

10.11. Where government proceeds with the *recapitalization of a bank without changing the management team* responsible for its failure, the most likely outcome will be for the same problems to recur as struggling and delinquent borrowers are granted fresh loans, recovery procedures remain ineffectual, operating costs continue at pre-rescue levels and internal controls continue as unreliable as ever. Worse still, this situation creates a perverse incentive for bad management, inasmuch as more losses may elicit further government recapitalization.

11. 'False friends' are also to be found in the area of *bank privatization*. In itself, privatization is a sound policy, which encourages competition, more effective management and market discipline under the right conditions. Nevertheless, it can also prove a 'false friend'. Let us consider two examples.

11.1. Some governments opt to privatize insolvent banks without fully recapitalizing them first, and sometimes without any recapitalization at all. Limited recapitalization to the extent of the budgetary funds available is quite common, and in such cases it is usual for the authorities to declare publicly that losses have been entirely dealt with, rather than recognizing their true scale and seeking the necessary funding and financial arrangements to spread the fiscal loss over a number of years. The result is that banks are put up for privatization while they are still insolvent, or at least undercapitalized. This makes it much more difficult to find a sound, large and solvent institution to take on the role of new owner or strategic partner. Instead, undesirable candidates will be quick to appear. Such bidders care little about the solvency of the institution privatized, because they will end up getting a return and recovering their investment through dividends based on fictitious profits or through bogus loans to themselves and their agents. Insolvency will persist. Is this privatization a 'good friend'? Let us not forget that one of the main goals of privatization is to find sound owners or strategic partners who can ensure proper management in the future and prevent any recurrence of past problems.

11.2. Another example of privatization as a 'false friend' is the privatization of a still insolvent bank (as in the previous example) to the general public without first seeking a strategic partner and ensuring that a solid, experienced management team is in place. All kinds of surprises are to be expected in such circumstances, but it is particularly likely that undesirable shareholder groups will gain control of the bank, leading to the situation described in the previous example, while the government may find itself facing legal action for overpricing a public sale.

12. *Reorganization* can become a 'false friend' if measures are applied to insolvent institutions without simultaneous, or better yet, prior, recapitalization. The most competent managers in the world will eventually fall victim to the hydra of insolvency unless it is dealt with financially, and even the best systems and technologies cannot help rebuild an insolvent bank's equity. As a leading expert once said, reorganizing insolvent banks without recapitalization is 'like rearranging deckchairs on the Titanic'.

Note

The regulatory gaps described here are not just past history. On the contrary, they are present in most regulatory reforms, including those enacted after the 2008 international crisis, both at the national and international levels.

A very significant case of half-way solutions or 'false friends' is the regulation planned and issued by the European Banking Union in the present decade. Here are some examples:

Common supervisory and resolution mechanisms have been set up for the member countries, but a joint deposit guarantee scheme is missing. Common capital requirements are now in place, but they include questionable items. While appearing very demanding in terms of capital, the new rules neglect the assessment of assets and prompt provisioning.

5

The Dynamics of Undisclosed Insolvency

Undisclosed insolvency veiled in the accounts by cosmetic practices and borrowed
liquidity is rampant, a reality that can have devastating effects for bankers,
supervisors and the taxpayer alike.
A. de Juan

1. International experience tells us that banks tend not to disclose the reality of their solvency and results when they find themselves in trouble, resorting instead to creative accounting to keep up appearances. The result is that the general public, analysts, rating agencies and often enough even external auditors and supervisors remain blissfully unaware of their true situation, sometimes for years.

2. The model shown in the table headed *Dynamics of Undisclosed Insolvency*, which appears as paragraph 7, is inspired by the actual situation of a large number of problem banks and/or financial systems around the world, as observed by the author in situ.

3. The table reflects the difference between the financial statements (balance sheet and income statement) of a hypothetical problem bank as reported and as adjusted on the basis of sound accounting criteria and proper verification applied particularly in the areas of asset classification, provisions and income recognition. The model also shows the actual cash flows of the bank or financial system.

Excerpt from an article published in 2005 in *Revista de Temas Financieras*, a journal published by the *Superintendencia de Banca del Perú*, the Peruvian bank regulator. Jaime Caruana, then Governor of the Bank of Spain, published an article on Basel II in the same issue.

© The Author(s) 2019
A. de Juan, *From Good to Bad Bankers*,
https://doi.org/10.1007/978-3-030-11551-7_5

4. The chart summarizes the main balance sheet headings together with the hypothetical revenues and costs associated with each. An income statement is then added to reflect profit or loss and their distribution between taxes, retained earnings and dividends.

5. The column headed 'Cosmetic Accounts' reflects the image of the bank as it might be presented by any number of bankers experiencing difficulties as they seek to prevent the institution's true situation from becoming known and avert any instruction to recapitalize or other intervention by the supervisor. The goal is to buy time until some solution appears in the form of an upturn in the economy, windfall profits on high-risk transactions, the sale or merger of the bank, government assistance or some such favourable conjunction.

6. Let us now consider the figures reflected in the model, which shows a bank, or a banking system, with total assets of 100 monetary units (MU; to facilitate discussion of each item in percentage terms). The bank appears theoretically to be very liquid (10% of assets are held in cash), very well capitalized (equity is equal to 10% of total assets) and very profitable (pre-tax profit is 8.30% of total assets).

7. The dynamics of undisclosed insolvency are quantified in Fig. 5.1.

8. Regardless of other possible sleights of hand, the main cosmetic practice is to report 100% of the total loan portfolio (80 monetary units) as good and profitable. According to the information reported in the 'Cosmetic Accounts' column, then, there are no non-performing or bad assets. Hence, the portfolio of loans and securities generates a mean yield of 35% and no provisions or write-offs are required. The unfortunate reality that cannot be disguised, however, is the high level of operating costs (6% of total assets), which is twice the level of income from commissions (3%). Despite these high operating costs, no bad loans are recognized so the pre-tax profit is 8.3% of total assets, a stellar ratio beyond even the best banks in the world.

9. The model assumes that profits are conventionally distributed, so that 2.77 (or one third of profits) is paid as corporate tax, 2.77 (one third) is retained as reserves and 2.77 (one third) goes to the shareholders as dividends.

10. Let us now turn to the 'Adjusted Accounts' column, which shows how the financial statements might be restated to present a more faithful image of the bank's reality. Such adjustments are usually the result of new accounting standards or practices, tougher inspection and/or a stiffening of political will.

11. After adjustment, assets worth only 40 monetary units (out of 80 MU) are classified as good, generating a mean return of 35%. A further 20 units are treated as non-performing but recoverable at some time (e.g. delinquent mortgage loans). These loans generate no return and should be provisioned.

The Dynamics of Undisclosed Insolvency

Balance sheet	Cosmetic Accounts			Adjusted Accounts			Cash flows
	Volume	%	Income/Expenses	Volume	%	Income/Expenses	
Cash	10	0	0.00	10	0	0.00	
Property	10	0	0.00	10	0	0.00	
Loans and securities	80	–	–	80	–	–	
Good	80	35	28.00	40	35	14.00	
Non-performing	0			20	0	0.00	
Bad	0			20	0	0.00	
Provisions	0			(20)		–	
Total assets	**100**		**28.00**	**80**	**–**	**14.00**	**14.00**
Equity	10			10			
(Losses)	0			(20)			
Net equity	10	0	0.00	(10)	0	0.00	
Deposits	60	15	9.00	60	15	9.00	
Due to banks	30	25	7.50	30	25	7.50	
Total liabilities	**100**	**–**	**16.50**	**80**		**16.50**	**(16.50)**
Income Statement							
Financial margin			**11.50**			**(2.50)**	**(2.50)**
Commissions			3.00			3.00	3.00
Operating costs			(6.00)			(6.00)	(6.00)
Depreciation			0.20			(0.20)	
Provisions			0.00			(4.00)	
Total other income and expenses			**(3.20)**			**(7.20)**	**(3.00)**
Pre-tax profit/(loss)			**8.30**			**(9.70)**	**(5.50)**
Taxes			(2.77)			(2.77)	(2.77)
Retained earnings			(2.77)				
Dividends			(2.77)			(2.77)	(2.77)
Actual loss						**(15.24)**	**(11.04)**
At the end of the year simulated			New accumulated losses		(35.24)		
			New net equity		(25.24)		

Fig. 5.1 Financial statements versus reality, an experiential model

The remaining 20 MU comprise bad assets and losses. No income is recognized in respect of these items, which should be written off.

12. The adjustment of returns means that the financial margin is now negative (−2.5 MU). Meanwhile, the write-off of bad assets means the bank now has 10 MU of negative net equity, and the five-year schedule for the application of provisions for non-performing assets requires a charge of 4 MU to the income statement, resulting in a pre-tax loss of 9.7 MU. Actual cash flows are likewise negative (−5.50 MU).

13. Despite this red-ink reality, the bank continues to report the profits shown in the table, and it therefore also continues to pay taxes and distribute dividends. This only adds to the actual losses and negative cash flows on its business, increasing the adjusted loss to 15.24 MU and cash flow to −11.04 MU. Accumulated losses after only one year without corrective action are now 35.24 MU.

14. The hypothetical bank or financial system is, then, neither liquid nor solvent, and still less profitable. While it keeps on massaging the reality in its financial statements, however, the bank will be able to stay liquid by taking deposits from the public and seeking loans from other banks, and sometimes even from the central bank. This is achieved on the one hand by creative accounting and on the other by a willingness to pay high rates of interest on deposits and other liabilities. When its sources of liquidity finally run dry, the bank will have lost its equity several times over, and the government will be forced to take action even though it is now too late, so that resolution becomes much more difficult, costly and traumatic than early corrective action would have been.

15. As the model plainly shows, then, if insolvency, whether in a bank or in the financial system as a whole, is not candidly disclosed and problems are not addressed, and if the public and analysts are shown only the situation reported in the cosmetic financial statements, then any apparent compliance with minimum equity rules and market controls will be an illusion, based on the analysis of information reported by the banker that is not only insufficient but in all likelihood misleading and possibly even counterproductive.

Note

While based on solid experience, this is a theoretical model based on events that have recurred in the past and will do so again in the future, whenever banks and supervisors fall prey to the problems described in this book.

6

Obstacles to Crisis Resolution. Excerpts from the Paper 'Clearing the Decks'

Even where strong bank supervision and a sound institutional framework exist,
the resolution of insolvent banks may meet many obstacles.
A. de Juan

Fear of moral hazard can be paralyzing and must be moderated. It is not
inevitable and it can sometimes be the lesser evil.
A. de Juan

1   Obstacles to Crisis Resolution

When a bank is insolvent, it should be recapitalized by the previous owners or new partners, or it should be closed unless the authorities decide that it is viable or that closure could trigger a wider crisis. Many governments adopt a general policy of never closing any banks. This may be utterly wrongheaded, but no matter, they adopt the policy anyway. In other cases, banks are neither closed nor effectively restructured, but rather because of the many obstacles in the way of resolution than any general policy.

Excerpt from the paper *Clearing the Decks*, delivered at the World Bank's fourth annual Banking Conference on Development in Latin America and the Caribbean, held in El Salvador in June 1998. The Conference was attended by Joseph Stigliz, who has since been awarded the Nobel Prize, and Stefan Ingves, the current Governor of the Central Bank of Sweden and Chairman of the Basel Committee.

1.1   Fiscal Discipline

The desire to protect taxpayers is one of the commonest obstacles, though this attitude is far from realistic. To illustrate this, let us consider the following dialogue between a government (G) and an advisor (A), which, though fictional, might almost have been 'transcribed' by the author from his real-life experience:

A: In cases of insolvency, the key is to provide real capital. The problem cannot be resolved by means of loans, however they may be structured, or by refinancing, subordinated debt or any other such arrangements. And of course, creative accounting, fancy financial engineering and all of that is no use whatsoever.

G: I understand all that. Mind you, the previous owners will always refuse to throw good money after bad.

A: Yes, I can see that. Close the bank then. Or if you really can't close it, then recapitalize it officially with public funds and any finance industry contributions you might need. But make sure you write off the existing capital first, so as to remove the previous owners and management and forestall any moral hazard. Once you have gained control of the bank, you can sell it on to a healthy institution.

G: That all sounds fine, but where are we going to find the capital to recapitalize and restructure a bank? There are no budgeted funds available for such a measure, and we simply cannot loosen fiscal discipline. The international bodies would kill us. So, let's wait for a liquidity crisis, and then we can use the central bank's last resort facilities. Maybe we could keep rolling over short-term facilities. Who knows, they might even be repaid someday. But it's really no matter, because any fiscal loss on these loans will take time to arise, and what we need now is to gain time.

A: I'm sorry, but you must know that when a bank becomes illiquid and stays that way for more than a few weeks, it will probably have been insolvent for quite some time, and the hole is most likely very deep and growing deeper. So the problem has to be addressed for what it is, by providing capital as I have said. This can be done by injecting fresh capital or by carving out impaired assets and allowing a third party, either the government or a financial sector vehicle, to absorb the associated losses. It doesn't matter whether you use cash funds or government securities, providing they are highly liquid in the market. And of course, we are talking about a large enough volume of capital to generate actual profits and positive cash flows, and not just about a cushion against possible losses.

G: This is impossible. I've said that printing money or increasing the deficit is out of the question. And having the central bank take the hit would be absolutely beyond the pale as well. There is only one way around the problem: the government will have to announce formally that it has found that the bank's insolvency is 'manageable'. Suppose we 'decide' that the sum of accumulated losses to be written off 'cannot' be more than the budgetary funds available for restructuring. Then we could allocate funds for the amount of the necessary write-downs and, hey presto, problem solved. It really doesn't matter if there are still some losses to be dealt with. Time will take care of that. Naturally, we would make an official statement to assure the public that the problem has been fixed. Announcements of that kind will restore confidence and ensure that we get international support and gain the time we need. The next elections might even bring in a new government and let us pass the problem on.

A: If you do that, you've had it. As long as the banks conceal their true situation and stay artificially liquid, their losses will grow exponentially with disastrous effects. The increasing cost of financing non-performing assets is a case in point, relentless pressure to use new deposits and loans to cover general and administrative expenses, which eventually strangles credit and results in pyramid lending, misallocation of resources to the worst debtors and worsening moral hazard. And of course, the fiscal bill will grow apace, not to mention the harm done to jobs and the economy.

G: So you really think we're lost? Don't you think economic growth will provide a solution? We do. And, our successors will know how to fix these problems.

A: Kidding yourselves by putting your faith in the passage of time and doing nothing is the worst policy you could adopt. Once insolvency takes hold, losses will race ahead of growth in both the finance industry and the wider economy, like the hare and the tortoise. Expecting debtors' ability to pay to improve is moonshine. Don't you realize that the loss is already in the system, whether it is recognized or not? And what's more, you're are already coughing up huge amounts of money, just in other ways, like last resort loans, refinancing bank loans made to state corporations, subsidies paid to both banks and their borrowers. Why don't you work out a really well-structured package based on all of these forms of support so that you can apply them more rationally and effectively? What you're doing now has costs, but it has no benefits.

G: We beg to differ. What you want would bankrupt our financial system.

A: Just listen for a moment, please. I am not bankrupting your system. Your system is already bankrupt, whether I say so or not, and whether you recognize it or not. And it was bankrupted by its own managers, sometimes with the government's active or tacit connivance. All I am doing is to suggest you wake up and get a grip on the situation. What is at stake here is economic stability and growth, and the proper functioning of the payments system. The more you drag your feet, the costlier it will be. As the French say, 'You can't make an omelette without breaking eggs.' Obviously, stabilization can only come at a price, the same as protecting depositors (who have, by the way, already lost enough by your negligent supervision). Stop pussyfooting around! There is no magic bullet.

I invite you to do three things: first, take on the conventional wisdom in the areas of fiscal and monetary policy; second, use your imagination to mitigate, spread and/or offset fiscal and monetary impacts, since they are unavoidable; and third, create the institutional mechanisms you need to ensure effective restructuring.

1.2   Institutional Problems and Coordination

It sometimes happens that the right institutions and regulations do not yet exist when restructuring measures are adopted for the first time, which can create uncertainty among the principals with regard both to the actions required and the role of each. In general, the institutions in charge of the system will be the department of the treasury or equivalent ministry and the central bank or the banking authority where supervision is assigned to an independent agency. Other specialized institutions may also exist to handle cases of failure and resolution, as is the case in the US. These institutions are often too poorly or clumsily coordinated, however, presenting an obstacle to effective action and expeditious decision-making. Turf wars may break out if one institution pushes itself to the fore in the restructuring process, though it is more common for everyone to pass the buck until the central bank is left holding the baby.

1.3   Legal Uncertainty

When government money is used to close or recapitalize insolvent banks, their owners should lose their investments and voting rights, and incumbent managers their jobs. Their interests, the interests of delinquent borrowers and those of some employees will inevitably be affected by the new owner's restructuring strategy. The losers' defence of their interests often leads to legal action against the authorities based on allegations of technical error, confiscation, political motivation, discriminatory treatment, corruption and so on. Hence, the authorities need the legal certainty provided by clear, well-designed legislation on the basis of which to adopt the sometimes harsh measures which may be needed to deal with the crisis. Among other matters, the legal framework must provide for the removal of former owners and managers, the acquisition and sale of the shares of failed banks and their assets, and it must confer the authority to set prices. Legal proceedings must also be conclusive and quick. In the absence of legal certainty, the authorities may feel that it is better not to admit to or do anything about problems.

It goes without saying that the former owners and management of restructured banks must be allowed to defend their interests, but preferably only after the event, because otherwise they will still be in a position to interfere and delay closure or resolution while they retain ownership rights and executive positions, causing further losses and disruption. In this regard, we may note that it is practically unheard of for governments to make the mistake of closing or restructuring a bank unnecessarily, based on an overly pessimistic diagnosis. In contrast, the error of keeping insolvent banks going is all too frequent.

1.4   Insolvency and Foreclosure

The laws governing insolvency and foreclosure, and the related legal procedures, are outdated in many countries and are not well suited to the special needs of financial institutions. Liquidation procedures are often drawn out and bureaucratic, so that the assets concerned may lose significant value as the process crawls on. Likewise, the enforcement of guarantees against delinquent debtors tends to be wearisomely slow and recovery rates are frequently low. Corruption too can sometimes be a problem. These issues pose serious obstacles to effective restructuring, which can only be fixed by legislation to reform the rules and procedures involved.

1.5   Too Big to Fail

Some banks are so large that they are not only very difficult to manage but also hard to control, supervise and close. In such cases, the very complexity of the consolidated financial statements may hinder any realistic diagnosis of the situation, even when the institution concerned is manifestly insolvent. And even if the bank's ills could be diagnosed, the upheaval which resolution or nationalization would inflict upon the system as a whole will often inhibit action by government or supervisors. Worse still, size means power, and a bank that is too big to fail may hold sway over the government and supervisory authorities, making it well nigh impossible for them to adopt the necessary corrective measures. Indeed, the supervisor may sometimes dance to the tune of such mammoth institutions. This has perverse effects on the market, as competitors demand equally indulgent treatment.

1.6   Failure of Political Will

This is probably the main obstacle to timely, thoroughgoing and effective measures to tackle crises. Failures of political will may be found at the level of both government and supervisors. Sometimes, the supervisor may indeed seek faithfully to discharge its duties, only to find itself instructed by the government to refrain from drastic measures or to turn a blind eye. Such failures of political will can render even the best regulations toothless and thwart both supervisory mechanisms and resolution tools.

There may be many reasons for political or supervisory pusillanimity, aside from those already mentioned, but the most important are as follows:

– The desire not to upset the political or economic applecart, even where the situation is already precarious and any success cannot last.
– The determination not to give the lie to earlier triumphalism or damage electoral prospects.
– A lame duck government that is unable to gain the political support it would need to take energetic measures.
– Finally, there is the desire to avoid hurting the interests of the government's friends and clients, especially where bankruptcy could entail more general systemic or industry risk, not to mention lobbying by borrowers with close ties to decision-makers. In such case, inaction may be a concomitant of corruption.

2   Some Remarks on Moral Hazard

Moral hazard plays an important role in many in many aspects of life. It is part of human nature. Basically, it means that people will behave perversely in a context of perverse incentives, often taking absurd risks. Moral hazard is sometimes a consequence of government policy, though fear of it in relation to financial systems can be overly simplistic, so that it comes indiscriminately to pervade banking regulations. The blame for moral hazard is almost always laid on deposit guarantee schemes and bank rescues. Nevertheless, more careful reflection on the issues may help clarify when moral hazard is a real danger and when it is not, and indeed when a present moral hazard is secondary to other considerations. This is very important, not only for legislators but also for bleary-eyed decision-makers sitting in all night meetings called to deal with banking crises, when the first and only priority is to 'staunch the bleeding'. Under such circumstances, the avoidance of moral hazard cannot be a matter of primary concern.

2.1   Moral Hazard and Bankers

Certain situations may encourage bad bankers to enter into high-risk transactions or engage in fraud, or to deploy the full panoply of professional malpractice in order stay afloat, paying swingeing rates of interest on liabilities when they are already bankrupt. This is all too likely to occur when the regulatory framework is lax and there is little to fear, offering a clear-cut case of moral hazard. It will not happen, however, if the banker believes beyond doubt that there is a real threat of official intervention, and that he may lose his investment, his bank and his social position, and that he could end up being dragged through the courts. Sadly, bankers lose little sleep over the possibility that depositors might lose their savings.

– Poor regulation and supervision produce moral hazard by allowing insolvency, insider lending and fraud to pass unchallenged. Where the legislative framework and supervisory arrangements are strong, however, problems can be quickly identified, allowing the authorities to demand that realistic provisions be set aside and dividends or management incentives curtailed, to close failed banks and write off their equity, and to oblige their shareholders and managers to leave the institution. In such cases, moral hazard will always be nugatory.
– Full or very high explicit deposit insurance can certainly create moral hazard. However, this may also be the case when there is no deposit protection at all, which often ends up meaning that deposits are fully guaranteed de facto. Whether explicit or implicit, full deposit insurance makes it difficult for supervisors to close banks because of the cost. And when bankers know that it is highly unlikely their bank will be closed, they may be tempted to

engage in risky business transactions and practices. This perverse effect does not appear when deposit insurance schemes are explicit and protect only a modest volume of deposits.

- Does bank restructuring foster moral hazard? If it consists merely of recapitalizing failed banks with no further implications for their owners and managers, then it most certainly does. This is also true when recapitalization is put off more or less indefinitely, whether due to lack of funds and muscular supervisory institutions or because of a failure of political will. If restructuring is timely, however, and is accompanied by the removal of former owners and managers, and especially where wrongdoers may face legal action, then bankers will be at pains to manage their banks properly. In such circumstances, the threat of government action suddenly becomes credible. What seemed a paper tiger suddenly has teeth.

- Last resort lending will not cause moral hazard if terms are short and the loans are for moderate amounts, just enough to cover occasional and temporary liquidity shortfalls. This is no more than standard practice in any banking system. Rather, the risk will raise its head where regulations or local practice allow the amount of such liquidity support to go on rising and maturities are rolled over indefinitely. In these circumstances, the bad banker will notice that the central bank does not always demand adequate guarantees for long-term support and goes on committing ever more funds to save his institution. This actually makes the banker's position vis-à-vis the central bank stronger. 'Too late. Close the bank now if you dare.' A really bad banker may even be tempted to use the funds obtained to finance his own personal interests in such circumstances.

2.2   Moral Hazard and Depositors

Moral hazard affects depositors where regulation and supervision persistently fail to detect and resolve problems, deposits are 100% protected and governments never close failed. In such circumstances, it is only natural that depositors should put their money in the banks that pay the highest interest without any further thought. These are probably the worst banks, paying high interest to stay 'physically' liquid and so survive while concealing their underlying illiquidity and insolvency. Depositor moral hazard will be much less where deposit insurance is limited. It is after all intended only to inspire the necessary confidence in the market and to prevent major social catastrophes, and in this light its existence may be considered a reasonable trade-off.

The same could be said of 100% deposit protection in cases of resolution. If restructuring prevents systemic contagion, depositor moral hazard may in any event be considered a minor evil.

It might be asked, meanwhile, whether depositors, who normally have access only to limited and not very reliable information, are ever in a position to tell a good bank from a bad one. Considering that rating agencies, investment bankers, auditors and even supervisors are also sometimes quite wrong in their diagnoses and that the candid disclosure of problems is a chimera, how can depositors in fact ever be expected to decide correctly which banks to trust with their savings?

2.3 Moral Hazard and Creditors

Much of the above discussion of uninsured depositors is also valid where a bank's creditors are protected from the consequences of failure de facto via restructuring measures designed to ensure the continuity of the institution. Creditor risk will be largely removed, however, where the possibility exists that all or part of the subordinated debt and other claims held may be written down or swapped for longer term debt or equity as part of a restructuring scheme.

2.4 Moral Hazard and Supervisors

Supervisors will not be exposed to moral hazard provided regulation is strong, analysts and bank examiners are well qualified and effective, the sanctions regime is strict, and policies with regard to closure and restructuring are realistic and placed in the hands of effective institutions. Where the obstacles described in this chapter exist, however, supervisors may step back from identifying solvency and other problems affecting the banks in their charge in case they are left holding the baby.

Supervisors may also be affected by moral hazard when their earlier actions in difficult situations were lax or flawed, which may make them reticent to identify or address problems that would highlight past errors.

7

The Financial Systems and the Ethics of Restructuring

*Lack of transparency constitutes a breakdown of good governance especially when
it is tolerated by the supervisor.
Where flagrant, it could also be considered a fraudulent practice.*
A. de Juan

I am neither an economist nor a philosopher, nor yet a specialist in business ethics. I read Law at university, and I am a banker by profession. From this privileged position in the trenches, I have had plenty of opportunity to learn at first-hand about the workings of the economy. And about people. This experience has allowed me, among other matters, to observe the behaviour of bankers, bank employees, supervisors and auditors in the complex, interdependent world of finance.

I have no mind to sit in judgement over other people here, for I am no judge. Nor do I pretend to believe that everything can be 100% perfect in this life, and that goes for banking too. Nonetheless, I would like to offer a critique of what I have seen with my own eyes.

When I told my oldest son the other day that I was coming here to deliver an address on the subject of banking ethics, he laughed and said, 'That's going to take about a minute, because you'll say that banking ethics have suffered tremendous damage and that will be the end of your speech.'

Lecture given at a seminar held at Fundación ETNOR in Valencia on 26 October 2011, with Adela Cortina, Professor of Ethics, sharing the floor and acting as moderator.

© The Author(s) 2019
A. de Juan, *From Good to Bad Bankers*,
https://doi.org/10.1007/978-3-030-11551-7_7

Well, no. I am not going to end in one minute and I hope to hold your attention for considerably longer. Rather than confining myself to ethics in relation to bank restructuring and in the different approaches, phases and procedures concerned in the process, I would like to begin with the behaviour observable in the lead-up period. Our question then is how crises happen and what stages of the process can be examined in ethical terms. In particular, I would like to highlight the matter of transparency, not just in the actions of banks and their managers, but also in the doings of auditors and supervisors, which also deserve consideration. Only then will I turn to the ethical aspects of restructuring *per se* to ask two key questions: Is it ethical to close down banks? And, is it ethical to keep them going?

1   The Build-up to Crisis

Banking crises may have both macro- and microeconomic causes. Macro causes might include international contagion, crisis in one or more sectors of the economy, for example, the property industry, and sharp changes in the price of oil or other key commodities. However, crises can also be caused by microeconomic or institutional factors. For example, we might mention excessive indebtedness in wholesale markets resulting in an overnight freeze, allocation of credit en masse to borrowers who cannot repay their loans, and the lack of proper controls and corrective measures. Meanwhile, weak regulation and inadequate supervision can also create the conditions, if not the trigger, for crisis. A lack of transparency, meanwhile, will only aggravate these factors by preventing early recognition of adverse realities and timely decision making.

One special feature of the financial industry, compared to others, is that insolvency comes first and only then illiquidity. To put this another way, when a bank has been illiquid for few months, it is safe to say that it has actually been insolvent for several years, and that the extent of its insolvency has increased. By conveniently massaging its accounts and paying interest at high rates, however, an institution will be able to go on attracting deposits even if its business has become a sham. This is the opposite of industry, where illiquidity comes first, only then leading to bankruptcy, when it will be up to the courts to establish whether or not the firm concerned is actually insolvent.

Insolvency is the culmination of a process involving multiple stages, however. We need to ask, then, how it is possible to be a good banker one minute and a bad banker the next. Let us imagine a sound, competently run bank, which makes good loans, earns healthy profits and distributes dividends, and treats both its employees and its customers properly.

One day, however, our bank's managers commit a series of technical blunders, which might happen to any of us. These mistakes may be caused by incompetence, failure to adapt to change or even by a sharp deregulation of business conditions.

Such technical errors do not, of course, deserve any negative ethical judgment. They are simply mistakes. Nevertheless, they may knock the balance sheet out of kilter, causing the bank to take on more debt and increase its leverage. Lending becomes concentrated in ever more doubtful customers and vulnerable sectors of the economy, so that recovery is no longer assured. The bank's bottom line suffers, and both equity and liquidity are affected. In order to drum up liquidity, it raises the return on deposits, which only feeds back into the loop of deteriorating profits. However, the situation is not yet hopeless—these are after all only technical issues. What is the remedy? It is for the shareholders and senior executives openly to admit the situation, to inject fresh capital and to replace failed managers. Meanwhile, the market must be persuaded that corrective action is being taken. Admitting the truth raises rather than undermines confidence.

Instead of openly admitting problems and changing their management approach, however, some bankers prefer to play for time, hoping that a solution will soon appear or circumstances will change, and at the same time seeking to prevent deposit outflows or any fall in the share price. They may also be keen to keep their jobs, given high executive pay and social status. The next step is to cook the books. This does not correct the problem, but sweeps it under the carpet. Who is likely to be behind such practices? In the first place, we find the shareholders and the bank's own managers, who set policy and sign off the accounts. Auditors and supervisors often fail to pick up on creative accounting, however.

Managers will fiddle a bank's accounts for the reasons already mentioned. But why do auditors put up with it? Auditors play a key role and often lock horns with managers over transparency issues. Sometimes they fold, however, giving up the constant struggle against 'creative' accounting. There is an underlying conflict of interest for auditors here. Who do they actually work for? Who are they supposed to tell that an organization's financial statements are or are not reliable? In the end it is the client, whom the auditor will always be keen to retain. Auditors may also misconstrue the nature of their mandate. Traditionally, auditors were required to say whether an organization's financial statements presented a 'true and fair' view of its financial and business situation. More recently, however, a new concept has been added which, though good in itself, can have undesirable consequences. Auditors are now also required to express an opinion on the future outlook of the institutions audited. The projections and plans prepared for these purposes may be based on a bullish depiction of present circumstances, which neither management nor the auditors are inclined to correct. This could be seen as a misinterpretation of the audit mandate. However, the failure to pick up on skewed reporting may also be due simply to lack of expertise on the part of more junior auditors. It is common enough for audit firms to offer low fees as a sweetener to win engagements, and then to economize by assigning less experienced professionals to the audit team. Pressure may also come from political quarters or, rather more rarely, from the supervisory authorities themselves if they are eager to cover up an unwelcome reality.

It may also be that supervisors simply overlook transparency problems, either because of weak regulation which does not allow them a sufficient legal basis to demand compliance, or because of their own lax application of the rules. Such cases almost always involve an overly optimistic view of both the economic outlook and the business itself.

In my own opinion, a supervisor can prudently allow a reasonable degree of indulgence in the short run, provided both the wider economy and the business are improving. However, such tolerance is suicidal if any deterioration is expected in either the economy or in a bank's business, because it will only hasten the organization's decline. Yet this does not seem to be widely understood. Meanwhile, the toleration of problems may sometimes reflect a lack of determination on the part of the supervisory authority or a failure of political will.

2   Let Us Now Turn to the Matter of Accounting Malpractice

How are the books actually cooked? There are of course myriad different recipes, but I will focus here on one of the commonest, which is often the most important in terms of consequences. This is to refinance doubtful loans, which is usually done by extending the repayment period and funding fictitious interest payments by the borrower, thereby ensuring the continuation of 'evergreen' loans. 'You owe me principal of one hundred on my loan plus eight in interest. But don't worry, I'll make you another loan for one hundred and eight with a longer repayment schedule, so you'll be able to pay me back (?) the interest.' It may be said without fear of contradiction that the worst loans, those that are large and rotten enough to sink a bank, are almost never classified as in default but are treated as normal. As a result, no provisions are made and interest accruals are not suspended. This means that a part of profits, provisions, new reserves and equity are actually fictitious. This practice therefore blinds shareholders to the reality, leading them to believe that the situation of the business is positive so that they continue to buy and hold shares. It also misleads depositors, who continue to entrust their savings to the bank, not to mention the markets and supervisors. I leave it to you, then, to decide whether false accounting can be called ethical.

It is fair to say that tendentious financial reporting is not merely a technical accounting matter, but a grave ethical issue. It can also be a key factor in concealing an incipient crisis, in aggravating the situation and in delaying corrective action. Managers are accountable to shareholders; auditors are responsible to both shareholders and the market; and the supervisor is responsible to society as a whole for the transparency and stability of the financial system. Hence, it is a serious matter when problems are overlooked and no corrective action is taken. By failing to act, moreover, the supervisor also tacitly broadcasts a perverse message throughout the system: 'Do what you like, it doesn't really matter.'

We are now entering the next stage: the accounts are by now thoroughly misleading and no action has been taken to fix matters. A downward spiral now begins, in which ever more serious problems are created while none are resolved. As a banker, I do not want to recapitalize my institution in the normal way, replace second-rate managers or admit to the reality of my bank's situation, so I will see whether I can save myself by upping the stakes. This does not normally happen, however, for high risk remains high risk. The downward spiral can take many forms, but one of the most serious is the concentration of risk in zombie customers. This is because the withdrawal of a bank's support for a major customer who is already in dire straits is likely to trigger bankruptcy, and therefore swingeing losses for the bank itself. Though it is not inevitable, this can tempt bankers to lend ever more to already struggling borrowers. The downward spiral is also evident when an organization begins investing heavily in high-risk sectors—oil when there is an oil crisis, property when there is a property crisis. The idea is, 'Prices are sure to rise and then I'll be out of the woods.'

According to economic theory, high risk may be acceptable because it is compensated by higher interest rates, though this can prove chimerical. Be this as it may, it is usually the case in practice that banks which set high contractual interest rates attract unsound debtors in the first place and are less likely actually to collect the interest or, indeed, recover the principal loaned. Speculation is another downward step in the spiral. This involves buying an asset to resell it, because prices in the market concerned are rising fast. The fact is, however, that the bottom can easily fall out of such markets, that the returns to be had simply vanish.

This brings us to a last phase of ever more dubious practices. Let us begin with the spurious acquisition of treasury shares, a practice that is half way between an accounting fiddle and fraud. Where a bank is in difficulties, its stock is likely to fall, and its managers may then have it buy shares in the open market in order to shore up the share price and so defend their own personal wealth. This tactic also encourages investors to continue buying the shares, though at a price that no longer reflects their fair value. Meanwhile, significant holdings of treasury shares can also impair a bank's own equity because price no longer reflects actual value.

As if this were not enough, bankers use other people's money rather than the bank's own when they proceed in this way. In ethical terms, such practices can only be qualified as disgraceful.

We now arrive at the fifth stage of deterioration on the threshold of disaster, which is outright fraud.

As the end approaches, our banker finds that all of his efforts to stave off ruin, in no small part for his own benefit, have failed. The bank is now quite insolvent. Intervention and bankruptcy loom large, accompanied by interminable conflicts with shareholders and a tide of legal actions that will in all probability end only when the bank is finally wound up. All too often I have heard the plaintive excuse, 'It's not my fault. It's all down to the experts and politicians who run the economy, and the ones who have just got it in for me.' Then there are those who through gritted teeth proclaim 'Family comes first for me. I would do anything to defend my family.'

What is the nature of the frauds committed? There are countless possibilities, of course, but one is 'self-lending'. The banker grants loans to companies which he owns or controls either directly or indirectly, or through dummy companies and agents. He might also lift any liens securing such bogus loans, or put them in the name of straw men. Then the banker can arrange 'pendulum' transactions, using dummy companies to purchase high value assets owned by the bank at prices below their fair value. A company owned by the banker may also sometimes hold assets that have become impaired. In these cases, the banker sells the assets to his bank at inflated prices. There are many other formulas, of course. To begin with, there is the widespread practice of 'feathering one's nest' just in case by manipulating severance payments, remuneration and pensions. This must of course be done in good time to avoid the possibility of legal challenge. The ethics of the matter is never a consideration.

Where auditors and supervisors fail to put a stop to this raft of fraudulent practices, they are by default allowing the deterioration of the institution concerned to continue. In the end the costs will only be higher, and the taxpayer will have to foot the bill.

So much for the causes of insolvency, whether arising successively or in tandem. The question is now whether to restructure the ailing bank or to close it.

When, despite all the dilatory stratagems I have described, the truth finally dawns that a bank is insolvent there are just two options—closure or rescue.

Closure means withdrawing the institution's banking licence and the start of formal insolvency proceedings, and it may sometimes result in criminal prosecutions. Yet we may ask, is it ethical to close a bank? If the diagnosis is right and the bank is actually insolvent but the banker did nothing to set matters right and failed to respond to demands for corrective action from the supervisory authority, then closure must indeed be seen as ethically right. However, the fear of contagion, of what has now come to be called 'systemic risk', means that banks are actually very rarely closed, and then only in isolated minor cases. The default option is therefore normally rescue and restructuring. The ailing institution can be placed in the hands of another stronger bank capable of assuring its future. This is not intended to save the banker, but to save the payments system and depositors, not to mention preventing contagion to other banks. Rescue may require intervention by the supervisory authority, changing directors and executives, a change of ownership (which may be either spontaneous or inducted by the authorities), forced cost-cutting, and the placement or sale in the market of a controlling stake to institutions capable of completing the restructuring process. This is followed by the liquidation of bad assets carved out from the failed bank, either by the buyer itself or by a government agency, in order to ensure the success of the rescue. Additional capital may also be injected where necessary.

Let us now briefly address the different kinds of rescue and restructuring processes from an ethical standpoint.

Is intervention ethical? Is it right to remove a bank's directors and managers? The answer is that it must be where the objective is to halt further uncontrolled deterioration, limit the cost to the public purse, and prevent market distortions and fraud when an institution is in its last throes. This is because it is right to protect the payments system, depositors, bondholders, taxpayers and the economy in general where the risk of contagion exists.

Is it ethical to impair the value of shares held by a bank's owners, or even to strip them of ownership? Once again, the answer is yes. Let us see why. The value of shares may be impaired in several ways.

– If the stock is listed and investors perceive the bank's deterioration, a fall in the share price is inevitable. It is the law of the market and there can be no further discussion.
– Where the shares are not listed, the majority shareholders were responsible for or allowed the impairment of their own asset. They staked their interest in the institution and so lost it. Furthermore, it is usually the case that the controlling shareholders will already have fiddled themselves some form of compensation if the value of their shares falls, employing the kind of self-contracted transactions discussed above.

As to the shareholders' loss of ownership *per se*, the impairment of the bank's equity will have reduced its value to zero, or even less. Continued ownership by such parties would only worsen the situation.

Without wishing to enter into an exhaustive discussion, let us look briefly at the basic elements of rescue and restructuring operations. I shall begin with cost cutting. The key to cutting costs is to shrink the headcount. Are job losses ethical? Sackings are clearly right when the objective is to remove incompetent employees who hinder the effective running of the business, and to clear out any who may have been involved in malpractice. It may be, however, that jobs must be lost simply to ensure an institution's viability. Both early retirement and voluntary redundancy schemes, and indeed lay-offs, can be perfectly ethical, insofar as such procedures are the lesser of two evils where the very survival of an ailing bank is at stake. In other words, such schemes are right when the alternative may be closure of the bank and the loss of all, rather than just some, of the jobs it provides.

What does raise a serious ethical problem is the remuneration paid to the managers of insolvent banks, especially where they may already have received government assistance. It is true that the new directors and managers brought in to turn an ailing institution around deserve substantial compensation, but always within limits. The former managers, meanwhile, should either leave the institution or be paid subject to the strictest constraints.

Even so, problems of this kind can sometimes arise in banks that are operating normally, and the issue of executive pay has recently elicited general censure in the US and indeed worldwide. What possible solutions could there be? There is one strong argument that is habitually made not just by bankers but by business people in general: if executive remuneration is capped, firms will be prevented from capturing and retaining the best talent, which will eventually be detrimental to the corporate interest. Yet even this important consideration has its limits, and it remains necessary to avoid excessive or disproportionate pay gaps with rank-and-file employees.

Another key restructuring issue is the injection of public funds. Is it right for public institutions (in the last analysis the taxpayer) to inject cash to save an ailing bank? I would say it may be in order to save the system. However, such injections should entail the ineluctable condition of a change of ownership and management. It is simply wrong to inject cash into a bank to the benefit of the very owners and managers who caused or allowed its deterioration. And this is so for reasons both of ethics and effectiveness.

Another key restructuring measure is loan recovery. Should we sympathize with bad debtors? Is it ethical to pile further pressure on those who are already struggling to repay loans? Let us not forget here that the money a bank lends is not its own but was entrusted to it by depositors in good faith. Accordingly, the institution is obliged to recover and return their funds. Furthermore, the collection of debts lies at the heart of commercial life. Indeed, one of the basic tenets of Roman law is *'pacta sunt servanda'*, meaning 'agreements must be performed', or more loosely, 'my word is my bond'. A loan constitutes a contract, and it is ultimately backed by the borrower's word. Moreover, failure to recover loans creates perverse incentives in the market for both lenders and borrowers, encouraging a culture in which 'nobody collects and nobody pays'. This spells only ruin for the system. Lenders will become negligent in their lending policy, while borrowers will ask for more than they actually need and will baulk at repayment with impunity.

A final issue is the liquidation of assets, which should be undertaken under the best possible conditions of competition, price and terms. However, this does not mean that cronyism and even corruption do not sometimes prevail. This is evidently wrong in ethical terms.

These remarks are based on my experience as a banking professional and not on any qualification as an ethicist.

8

Liquidity and Euphoria

Excess liquidity dulls the banker's sense of risk, encourages reckless growth and may even end in insolvency.
A. de Juan

Hanging on the wall of a senior official at the Bank of England, I once saw a framed copy of the 'Advice to Bankers' written in 1863 by Hugh McCulloch, at the time Comptroller of the Currency and later US Treasury Secretary. This pithy letter sets out nine basic principles. Not a line of his advice is wasted, either for his contemporaries or for today's bankers. Among other trenchant counsel, he ordains, 'Never renew a note merely because you may not know where to place the money with equal advantage if the note is paid.'

Last December the European Central Bank (ECB) issued an alert with regard to a 'wave of leveraged acquisitions of listed companies'. Indeed, it did so twice in the space of one week, warning that 'this wave could have implications for the health of the banking system' and recalling that similar phenomena in the US had ended in a slough of bankruptcies with adverse impacts on the economy as a whole. The ECB further noted that lending to business had expanded in the autumn, at its fastest rate since the institution's creation in 1999. Meanwhile, business indebtedness in the EU had grown from 135% of gross domestic product (GDP) to 165%. Other European central banks are even now urging bankers to lend at prudent rates and to show caution in their risk assessments.

Article published in the Spanish economic daily *Cinco Dias* on March 2007, four months ahead of the international liquidity crisis unleashed in July of that year.

© The Author(s) 2019
A. de Juan, *From Good to Bad Bankers*,
https://doi.org/10.1007/978-3-030-11551-7_8

On 19 January, the *Financial Times* (FT) published fragments of a letter from a senior executive of a British bank, who also had some interesting things to say. 'I have never seen anything like what is happening now.' 'The market seems to have forgotten what risk is and is behaving as if the so-called "wall of liquidity" will last forever and volatility were a thing of the past.' 'I do not believe that there has ever been a time in history when such a large proportion of the riskiest assets were held by such weak institutions... with such scant capacity to withstand any events that might have a negative impact on the availability of credit or any downturn in the market.' The banker concludes, 'I am not sure which is worse, talking to "market players", who usually believe that "this time it's different", or talking to old hands who admit in private that there is a bubble and it must burst sooner or later, but who only hope that there will be no problem ... until they can collect their next bonus.' It is indeed true that the international economic outlook looks bright and that the 'fundamentals' look sound. This might perhaps justify a degree of optimism in risk assessments, but optimism is not what we are seeing today.

It is obvious that the duration of the economic cycle has changed and that the present abundance of liquidity may lead to riskier lending policies and the relaxation of risk controls based on rigorous analysis of potential borrowers. This is likely especially if banks become overly keen to place the funds currently sloshing around in the market in order to assure strong growth in their volume of business and profits, and all the more so if such policies are combined with a determination to keep the share price high and so 'add value for the shareholders', or where loans are made primarily to strengthen a bank's relative position as buyer or target in possible mergers and acquisitions, seeking a more favourable exchange ratio and share-out of power after a transaction is completed. It is easily forgotten in this context that it is not the return *on* equity reflected in the books, but the actual return *of* equity in reality that is important, as a traditional banker once said to me.

Given the abundance of cheap money, international banks offered, not to say pressed, huge loans on business and governments in highly risky countries. The receivers of this credit were only too happy to accept, regardless of whether the funds were subsequently put to good use or bad. They were of course aware that the loans would be difficult to repay, but their thinking appears to have been, 'It's up to lenders to measure their risks, so it's their problem.' Events then took their inevitable course.

Personally, I cannot forget the consequences of the 'credit orgy' in Mexico in the 1990s following a round of bank privatization that was to a great extent financed by lending to the buyers. And that is just one example. It is a classic rule of good banking that credit growth should be consistent with the growth in deposits taken from third parties and should not be too dependent on other more volatile sources of finance. This principle seems now to have been almost buried beneath the mass of interbank liquidity and range of financial products available in the market. Yet it remains a basic guide to policy.

Furthermore, the superabundance of liquidity has driven the volume of loans granted to large borrowers to unprecedented heights in absolute terms. There is no shortage of bankers who believe that maximum limits should be generous if a client is creditworthy, and that the case-by-case examination of loans is secondary. Moreover, mere inertia makes it unlikely that credit limits will be reviewed until it is too late.

What can we say of the securities markets? Stock markets have been rising without pause, successively breaking previous records. This trend is based in part on the strong performance of most firms and on low interest rates. However, it is also partly down to acquisition fever both within and across industries. To the extent that this is an actual fever and not a normal market phenomenon, we may observe situations in which major firms coveted by investors have doubled their stock market value in little over a year and have distributed succulent dividends, although neither their size nor their performance could possibly justify such outrageous increases either in the share price or in pay-outs. In any event, the prevailing climate of market euphoria only spurs on the protagonists of such transactions and onlookers alike. The watchword is, 'There's still room for growth.' A key feature of this panorama is that some of the principal mergers and acquisitions in question are actually financed with bank loans, and both the principal and interest will one day have to be repaid. This may seem obvious, but we should ask ourselves whether the targets and buyers in these transactions will ever produce high enough returns to service their debts. What if they fail? In that case, buyers would still have a way out through speculative sales of their new shareholdings. But if these cannot be sold at a high enough price, then we may easily imagine the impact on the transparency of the buyer's—and maybe the financier's—financial reporting.

One can only wonder about the investment banks' role in all of this. Their current growth is extraordinary all over the world. Evidently, this is partly due to the current M&A fever, in which they are active players. It might also be asked, however, whether the investment banks are not 'stoking' the market to benefit their own business.

Let me refer briefly here to a factor which could complicate matters enormously, namely, the likelihood that the new international rules known as Basel II will lead to a lowering of minimum capital requirements and the probable insufficiency of the provisions made in no small number of financial systems. This is due basically to the questionable parameters established in the Basel II rules for the measurement of equity and to the application of ever laxer risk verification mechanisms by bankers and supervisors alike given the scope for self-regulation allowed by the new rules.

All of these questions are key to the stability of our financial systems, even without adding the hoary though no less important matter of mortgage lending to the mix. To paraphrase Karl Marx's definition of religion, I have always believed that liquidity is the 'opium of the banker' and, indeed, of the supervisor. In this light, allow me if you will to end these remarks with a question: what will happen when the economy runs into trouble? Above all, what will happen when the tide of liquidity runs out, leaving the markets high and dry?

9

The Recommended Option

The ideas for ways to address the recent international crisis in Spain described in this article were informally presented by the author to the authorities and were received with interest. However, they were never applied.
Somebody who knows the Spanish savings banks very well said at the time, 'The savings banks are divided into those that are in trouble and those that are in deep trouble.'
The influence of regional governments, overoptimistic diagnoses and forecasts, and fiscal short-termism initially resulted in feeble enforcement of the rules and the tardy and costly application of ineffective solutions, like the creation of a new resolution entity, the so-called 'cold mergers' between ailing savings banks and very insufficient initial recapitalization, instrumented by means of debt issues rather than by issuing of share capital, which was only done a few years later.
A. de Juan

The Spanish resolution entity was set up in June of the same year and only began its work two years into the crisis, by partly financing the merger of poorly assessed entities with costly securities.

There are three deposit guarantee schemes in Spain, one for each of the three parts of the country's financial system—banks, savings banks and credit cooperatives. The schemes were first set up in 1980 and, although they were incorporated as public law entities, their activities are governed by private law.

Article published in the financial daily *Expansión* on 26 March 2009.

© The Author(s) 2019
A. de Juan, *From Good to Bad Bankers*,
https://doi.org/10.1007/978-3-030-11551-7_9

During the crisis of the 1980s, the deposit guarantee schemes were equally financed by private institutions and the Bank of Spain. The governance of each scheme is entrusted to a management board formed by representatives of the financial institutions and the Bank of Spain in equal numbers. These boards have, however, always remained under the ultimate control of the latter through the casting vote held by the chair, who is the Deputy Governor of the Bank of Spain in each case. Since 1996, the schemes have been financed solely by the financial institutions, as required by European Union (EU) legislation. Nevertheless, the Bank of Spain can still contribute funds in 'exceptional circumstances' potentially affecting the stability of the system as a whole, subject to legislation expressly authorizing such funding.

According to the Act of the Spanish Parliament which created them, the deposit guarantee schemes serve a dual purpose, which is, on the one hand, to assure deposits below a given limit (currently €100,000) in the event of closure and, on the other, to finance the restructuring of insolvent institutions and even to absorb losses, where such measures would be less costly for the schemes or the financial system as a whole than to proceed with the closure of failed entities.

These institutions played the leading role in restructuring dozens of financial entities in Spain in the 1980s. A short decade later, they rescued Banesto applying practically the same tools, although mainly private capital on that occasion, almost all of it provided by Spain's banks. Meanwhile, the rescue and nationalization of the 20 banks belonging to the Rumasa Group were undertaken jointly by the Spanish financial system and the government, although management of these entities was placed in the hands of the bank deposit guarantee scheme, *Fondo de Garantía de Depositos en Entidades de Crédito*.

All of the banks rescued using the deposit guarantee scheme's or government money were sold on to new owners and were placed under new management as a matter of principle. 'There's no such thing as a free lunch', as the saying goes. And '[n]o pain, no gain', to boot.

The mechanism applied to change ownership of the banks was to reduce their share capital, which eliminated or severely diluted the stakes held by the former shareholders, while the deposit guarantee scheme subscribed a capital increase to complete an 'accordion transaction' (capital reduction and subsequent increase).

Meanwhile, management was changed by obliging the banks' directors to resign at the beginning of the restructuring process and replacing them with new, professional managers, recruited in all cases from the market. In those cases where a failed bank's directors refused to resign, they were immediately fired as soon as the deposit guarantee scheme was able to gain control of the institution. After appointing new boards, the deposit guarantee scheme proceeded in each case to recruit new executives and adopted 'surgical' measures to restructure management and facilitate the sale of the institution concerned. Where necessary, obdurate boards were removed pursuant to a decree of March 1978, which authorizes the Bank of Spain to take such action not only in private institutions, but also in the Spanish savings banks.

The main restructuring measures adopted by the deposit guarantee scheme, aside from the subscription of fresh capital, comprised the purchase of bad assets and absorption of the related losses, as the scale of the banks' implicit losses was more than their equity, while the share capital increases carried out were intended for recapitalization and were insufficient for this purpose. Bad assets were also carved out from the savings banks as a key recapitalization tool. To complete their financial restructuring, the Spanish deposit guarantee schemes also granted loans until the banks under their control returned to profit and could be sold off or merged. Some limited guarantee facilities were also awarded.

It proved impossible to agree a market price for bad assets with their former owners, and they were therefore purchased at face value (i.e. the nominal value of loans less provisions) in order to prevent the materialization of losses in the insolvent banks before they could be recapitalized. This meant losses could be materialized in the deposit guarantee scheme and could be definitively quantified a posteriori following the sale or liquidation of the related assets.

The legislation creating the bank deposit guarantee scheme allowed a maximum period of one year for the sale of failed institutions. In reality, however, all of the institutions restructured by the scheme were sold in an average of 13 months, including the Rumasa Group banks.

None of the banks rescued suffered a relapse after being sold, a reflection of the deposit guarantee schemes' effectiveness. Furthermore, as profitable institutions, they have generated significant revenues in the form of corporate income tax over the years since they were sold and placed under new management, and to a greater or lesser extent, this has offset the government financing received.

The restructuring of the Spanish savings banks was effected basically by means of merging struggling with larger, sound institutions under the stewardship of the Bank of Spain. Meanwhile, the savings banks deposit guarantee scheme (*Fond de Garantía de Depositos en Cajas de Ahorro*) purchased bad assets and made supplementary loans where it considered that rescuers would not be able to absorb the losses of failed institutions. Spanish savings banks do not have share capital as such, so the 'accordion' option of simultaneous capital reduction and increase was not available. In all of the operations in which the savings bank deposit guarantee scheme was involved, however, the acquirer of the failed institution first gained control of its board and management and then proceeded to remove or at least relegate former directors and managers.

The formal appointment of veto-wielding administrators was tried in a few cases, but failed. This formula was therefore discarded, as it created more problems than it solved. Such mechanisms may have some value for damage-limitation purposes while the search for a definitive solution is under way, but there remains a grave risk that serious problems will not be dealt with, and though the administrators appointed can veto or otherwise prevent malpractice in many cases, toxic transactions may still be completed behind their backs. I have seen this happen more than once. This means that it is beyond the ability of the administrators fully to discharge the responsibility laid upon them. Indeed, they may even be targeted in legal action taken by the institutions placed in their care and accused of malpractice or blamed for problems.

So much for the Spanish experience. My own professional observations in numerous countries have taught me to distinguish solutions that work from those that do not, or that only create more problems. In this context, I believe that the Spanish system of deposit guarantee schemes is a highly effective tool to address the ills of failing banks on a case-by-case basis for the following reasons:

- Deposit guarantee schemes benefit from a solid institutional, financial and legal framework, and they have demonstrated their effectiveness in practice without needing other instruments created *ex novo* or engaging in 'experiments', which can themselves present serious technical and political risks.
- The Spanish deposit guarantee schemes are no longer financed by government, but by means of annual contributions from the private-sector entities making up the financial system. These contributions could be further increased in case of need. Furthermore, ad hoc legislation could again allow the Bank of Spain, or indeed other official agencies, to provide additional funding in exceptional circumstances. Were such supplementary funds to be provided in the form of loans to the schemes or the subscription of debt issues, moreover, it would not be necessary to tap the public purse because the lender would eventually recover the sums in question from the deposit guarantee schemes out of the ongoing contributions required of the banks by law, not to mention partial recoveries of any bad assets acquired and the proceeds obtained on the eventual sale of any shares initially subscribed in problem entities.

- The deposit guarantee schemes have the capacity to ensure a change in the management and temporary control of problem institutions.
- They also ensure, by law, the sale of target institutions after rescue, or their direct merger with other institutions in a short space of time.
- As I have already mentioned, the Spanish deposit guarantee schemes thus constitute a version of the 'bad bank' concept, carving out bad assets from problem institutions and proceeding with their recovery or liquidation. The advantage is that they can acquire such assets at face value, thereby avoiding the enormous technical problems and possible litigious consequences of appraisal.
- The deposit guarantee schemes act on a case-by-case basis, which helps remove the suspicion that difficulties may be widespread throughout the system.

It is of course true that the Spanish deposit guarantee schemes are currently on standby, thanks to the financial bonanza of recent years. However, the institutional framework remains crystal clear, and it would be necessary only to provide a new, experienced, strong and independent management team for them to address any crisis that might arise. Furthermore, the collection or liquidation of bad assets could be entrusted to specialized institutions where necessary, given their volume or nature.

It is also true that the sale of any shares acquired by the deposit guarantee schemes would be difficult today given the small number of possible candidates to complete such acquisitions, and would probably take longer than one year, but this only means that it would be necessary to set the appropriate deadline in advance.

*   *   *

It goes without saying that measures to strengthen the financial system cannot by themselves end recession, which requires a whole raft of other fiscal strategies and direct official funding, not to mention structural policies designed to create a more balanced and diversified economy and ensure strong, competitive future growth. The fact remains, however, that economic recovery requires restructuring of the financial industry and the recovery of credit, without which things will not get better and could even get worse. Delay in adopting the necessary measures and artificial efforts to stoke an ailing economy may only undermine confidence, as we have recently seen. Meanwhile, the real economy and jobs will go on suffering for longer, which is no small matter in itself.

Of course, the initial measures adopted may have an adverse impact on public opinion and the markets, but they can also generate confidence if they are properly presented. This is a risk worth running, because effective solutions, if presented, will help ensure that the economy bottoms out sooner and that the green shoots of recovery will grow more vigorously when they appear. In any event, it is better to risk a bumpy ride at the outset than a head-on collision with reality in a couple of years' time.

Let me end with a question. In a matter of such transcendence for the economy as the recovery of the financial and credit system, could the mainstream political parties not set aside their usual partisan wrangles to seek consensus on the main thrust of the policies required?

Note

The mechanism described above was the author's recommendation to the Spanish government. What actually happened is described in Chap. 14, which is based on the testimony he gave in the Spanish Parliament in December 2017. As can be seen, the mechanisms initially applied were largely too weak to be effectual.

10

The Problems of the European Banking Union

The goal of all regulation ought to be to prevent insolvency, which would avoid costs for the taxpayer, disruption of the wider economy and job losses. Paradoxically, the new regulation focuses on ensuring a good 'burial', by alternative funding via the bail-in mechanism but only when a bank has already gone under. On the contrary, efforts to reduce the number of casualties were softened.

A. de Juan

The Banking Union is a major step towards strengthening the European Union. Though a single-deposit guarantee scheme has yet to be established, the Single Supervisory Mechanism (SSM) and Single Resolution Mechanism (SRM) are already in place. However, it would be foolish to sit back now and expect the new institutions to provide immediate solutions. They will not. Not in the Eurozone and not in Spain. They will take years to find their feet, in the first place making different regulatory systems converge is a difficult and a slow process and, in the second, because they have been set up even while the aftershocks of the financial crisis rumble on.

Let us recall that the policy measures implemented to deal with the crisis rested on the twin pillars of capital requirements, which have been sharply raised, and an expansive European Central Bank (ECB) monetary policy accompanied by low interest rates and easy terms. However, the emphasis on capital

Article published in the Spanish daily *El País* on 15 April 2016, criticizing the slow progress and reverses suffered by the new European mechanisms, the advent of which was considered by many to be a panacea marking the end of the crisis.

requirements seems to be designed primarily to fix problems after the fact. Perhaps even post mortem. Such measures fail to address the matter of prevention, basically because they do not bolster oversight of asset values, even though asset impairment was at the heart of the banking industry's sudden collapse and descent into crisis, while regulatory controls in this area were already undermined a decade ago by the new international accounting standards.

Regulatory requirements in any case validate certain capital components that are of poor quality and are questionable in conceptual terms, either because they are onerous or callable, or because they are devoid of economic substance or do not provide liquidity. Examples would include deferred tax assets (which remain a matter of concern even in Frankfurt), goodwill and certain hybrid securities such as the so-called contingent convertible bonds (CoCos), which are both costly and face an uncertain future.

The ECB's monetary policy is intended to combat deflation, and to foster lending and jobs. It reminds me of rediscounting, the classic last-resort lending tool. Indeed, the only difference seems to be that rediscounting facilities were granted only for very short terms to highly solvent institutions at steep interest rates. So far, the ECB's policy has barely attained its goals. However, it has now been extended sine die in order to buy time. This risks causing serious problems, by distorting banks' business, pumping up asset bubbles only to see them burst later on, weakening bankers' awareness of risk, papering over underlying problems, and perhaps exhausting the arsenal of measures with which to tackle future crises.

Meanwhile, reliance on these two pillars may blindside regulators to other key issues such as scant recurrent earnings, the murky quality of some assets (which could render the levels of capital and profits recognized in banks' financial statements entirely fictitious), imbalances resulting from excessive leverage in unstable wholesale markets, and the general malaise of inefficiency. The paradoxical consequence is that institutions beset by such problems tend to be treated as sound so long as they comply 'on paper' with the capital requirements set.

To my mind, supervision is more important than regulation, which is often lax, ambiguous or ignored in practice. In this light, the emphasis should be placed firmly on 'preventive medicine' in the form of stricter control in precisely those areas that have been overlooked. The key is to capture problems of decapitalization early on, so as to apply timely and effective corrective measures.

Meanwhile, the Single Supervisory Mechanism (SSM) is prey to its own problems. In the first place, these are a consequence of the inevitable differences in experience, culture and practice between the members of joint supervisory teams. According to the president of the SSM herself, around 50 of the 150 different regulations existing do not look likely candidates for convergence. So application will probably depend on the unequal criteria of national regulators, who are frequently influenced by (sometimes imperative) political considerations. The SSM could thus find itself forced to seek a common denominator among the feeblest regulations, eventually resulting in overly optimistic and tardy diagnoses. This is worrying.

It is particularly disturbing that the new inspections carried out under the aegis of the SSM rarely seem to quantify adjustments. Furthermore, the scant corrective measures demanded refer mainly to procedural matters. In fact, recent guidelines emanating from Frankfurt seek to avoid quantification of any kind and to ensure that inspections are completed in as short a time as possible, while focusing on the control of information processes.

In line with the general policy drift, the SSM has thus taken a further step towards relinquishing a key mechanism of effective supervision, to wit, the inspection of loan books to verify debtors' ability to repay their borrowings regardless of formal default rates, which is an easy indicator to massage. It has been said that such reviews are expensive, though in the end nothing is costlier than the lack of supervision. However, this key procedure has been increasingly replaced by other less reliable mechanisms like mathematical modelling and stress testing, even though such theoretical techniques have all too often been found wanting, based as they are on historic data provided by banks themselves and accepted without question. This ignores the reality that institutions are more likely to disguise problems the deeper their difficulties. And experience tells us that this can happen with the connivance of the regulator.

Good governance is the latest panacea. The concept is laudable, but its development is necessarily slow and difficult to control, because it requires the creation of a new corporate culture almost from scratch. For example, the SSM already oversees the make-up of banks' boards and their formal proceedings. Such measures fall short of the mark, however. Decisions are also taken outside the purview of the governing bodies, markets are manipulated, asset values are overstated, egregious management remuneration policies persist, and supposedly 'independent' directors may be swayed by the succulent rewards of their position.

Let us turn now to the SRM or Single Resolution Mechanism. Aside from the complexity and immaturity of the decision-making process, the kind of poor diagnosis I forebode could delay, handicap and eventually frustrate effective, early action to tackle bankruptcies.

There have been some unpleasant surprises of late, including Banco Espírito Santo (with total losses of 6.8 billion Euros), Monte dei Paschi di Siena (which has a 'declared' default rate of 40%) and Deutsche Bank (with losses of 6.9 billion in 2015 alone). The belated suddenness of these situations suggests that these institutions' difficulties were not identified in time either by the SSM or by national supervisors, despite the new regulatory framework and supervisory instruments created. What happened to the models, the stress tests and the famous asset quality review of 2014? It is clear that these problems were not addressed in time either by the SRM or the existing national mechanisms, which could have at least applied domestic remedies in their own countries.

To conclude, slow or erroneous diagnosis enormously increases treatment costs in cases of insolvency, which will have to be paid both by the financial system itself, and by creditors in the form of 'bail-ins'. Meanwhile, governments could easily find themselves once again involved, given the growing size of problems. Taxpayers beware! Meanwhile, the joint bail-out fund to be provided by the member states will be capped at 55 billion Euros, and in any case it will not be available until 2019.

Despite the new European arsenal of regulations, instruments and institutions, then, the key question remains, 'What would happen if a new banking crisis were to occur before the unified mechanisms reach maturity and can be effectively deployed?'

11

Stability and Its Risks

*Failure to address crisis or postponing appropriate action on the spurious grounds
of financial and political stability may only make matters worse and trigger
further upheaval.*
A. de Juan

In his youth, we are told, Augustine of Hippo, later Saint Augustine, found himself torn between high religious ideals and hedonism. As he himself famously wrote, his prayer was 'Lord, grant me chastity and continence, only not yet'.

These words put me in mind of the current situation of European financial systems. The response to the present financial crisis conveys the impression of a new regulatory and institutional fervour, a quasi-religious ideal, coexisting with a kind of hedonism, a marked coolness towards the actual application of the new regulatory framework. In other words, concern over general stability trumps diagnosis and treatment of the ills afflicting both the banking industry and the wider economy.

The crisis slouches on, and the hope that it will not flare up again is founded for many on the new regulatory and institutional framework that has finally been established. Its creators vehemently defend its pristine tools and preach its virtues to the world with apostolic zeal. The new regulatory armoury is indeed extensive. The relatively recent Basel III rules designed to correct the weaknesses of Basel II will soon be superseded by Basel IV, which is currently

---

Article published in the Spanish financial daily *Expansión* on 13 January 2017, focusing on the weaknesses of the European institutions in the face of aftershocks from the recent financial crisis.

in the pipeline. Then there is the European Banking Union founded on the pillars of regulation, supervision, resolution and, eventually, a common deposit guarantee scheme. The Banking Union was the result of efforts to standardize regulation, and the Basel Committee has successively raised the minimum equity banks must hold even while validating certain highly questionable capital components to help them toe the line. A parallel 'leverage' ratio has been created to compare equity with total assets. Meanwhile, 'internal' models and 'stress tests' have been deployed to establish the levels of equity required in different scenarios.

It is also planned to progress towards an initial concept of 'expected losses' in order to make capital estimates somewhat more realistic. Internal procedures for the control of loans have also been strengthened and efforts have been made to bolster good governance and improve bankers' conduct. Various joint supervisory teams have been created, run by the ECB from Frankfurt, to centralize the supervision of 129 major banks in the European Union. The European Banking Authority (EBA) periodically reviews asset quality. New audit laws have also seen enacted to tighten up review procedures.

The ECB has worked tirelessly to assert complex new resolution mechanisms. The newly established bail-in principle means that shareholders, junior bond holders and the holders of deposits in excess of €100,000 must now foot the bill for losses before taxpayers are called upon. Finally, negotiations are afoot to set up a common deposit guarantee scheme, despite the difficult consensus required to mutualize the costs. This is nothing short of a regulatory avalanche.

Reality goes on in a parallel universe, however, following its own immutable course. Eight years after the cataclysm unleashed by the collapse of Lehman Brothers, we can only look on as gigantic problems of insolvency and mismanagement surface in one country after another, affecting major banks with little or no prior warning. Germany, the United Kingdom, Italy, Portugal, Spain ... and the list goes on. Yet these difficulties were neither reported nor addressed in any meaningful way until they came to the attention of the markets. Worse still, such tardy and costly admissions of ruin raise the spectre that Frankfurt may yet endorse resolution mechanisms that fall short of or alter the formal framework created by the Banking Union, or which simply fail to tackle solvency issues, not to mention the vexed question of discriminatory treatment against banks operating in some countries compared to others.

Where were the business models, the stress tests, the periodic reviews of asset quality, the auditor effectiveness measures, the new capital requirements, the procedural controls and the alleged panacea of enhanced bank governance when they were needed? Suffice to say that all of these bids to strengthen governance are diametrically opposed to the spread of lavish remuneration policies among banks in general, and to a world in which supervisors are still prepared to tolerate the kind of whitewashing so typical of managerial misconduct. It would seem, then, that the existing national and international supervisory and resolution mechanisms are simply not working.

What is the reason for this disjunction? In the first place, it might be a matter of 'unintended consequences'. It could be, for instance, that the new rules and supervisory mechanisms have struggled to take hold where theoretical and qualitative tools were expected to replace the tried and tested quantitative procedures of direct supervision. Or it may be that the new regulatory and supervisory players as yet lack the necessary experience. It is also very likely a matter of perfectly logical inertia and teething troubles given the protracted implementation periods required and complex rollout of the new systems.

Such explanations cannot explain the whole picture, however. We are all only too well aware of the current vulnerability of our financial systems. Legacy problems in the property market have not yet worked themselves out. Banks' returns are at historically low levels, and the remedies for their lacklustre performance, such as digitization or mergers, are both slow and traumatic. Meanwhile, the threat of unregulated non-bank finance hangs like a black cloud over the financial industry, to say nothing of the broader qualms produced by ongoing political and geopolitical uncertainties.

In this light, we may posit the existence of other causes that are in fact actively driven by governments and supervisors. For example, the policy option adopted by no small number of countries has been to prioritize a simulacrum of stability, putting off any realistic diagnosis of problems and the early application of tough solutions. This may be because of a general fear that energetic action might uncover earlier failures in financial systems, opening up a Pandora's box of politically unwelcome risks and economically intractable difficulties. Such 'steady as she goes' policies are often preferred not only by governments, but also by major banks and lobbyists, all of whom may wish to avoid what has been dubbed 'intrusive' supervision in their countries and organizations. In the meantime, the reality of banks' liquidity and solvency can always be papered over by means of massive and indefinite monetary expansion at low or practically zero interest rates. This creates temporary stability, but the side effects can be grave, causing significant distortion in the banking industry as a whole. To paraphrase Saint Augustine, the prayer offered up by governments and bankers alike seems to be, 'Lord, grant us strong systems, only not yet.'

Such 'safe' policy may appear prudent to some. However, governments should take heed of the irrefutable truth that procrastination is always counterproductive when things are going badly, and when they take a turn for the worse. It can be suicidal. More than likely the stability prioritized today will turn out to be cosmetic and short-lived. If so, a new crisis could occur at any moment, bringing even greater costs in terms of economic, social and political upheaval. In that event, even those who avoided taking action when it was needed may count themselves among the victims in one way or another.

12

Practical Lessons for Dealing with Problem Banks

The worst loans are not recognized as being in default and are not provided for.
This is veiled decapitalization.
Benevolent diagnoses are more likely to be misleading than strict ones, and mild or
belated remedies are apt to prove costlier and more harmful to the economy as a whole.
A. de Juan

1   Introduction

History has a stubborn habit of repeating itself. Having worked in problem banks in four continents for over 40 years, I have distilled the practical principles, rules of thumb and, some might say, personal manias spelled out here. All of them belong to my own private world and they do not cover the areas of technological change and the new financial competition, focusing rather on the matter of solvency. Furthermore, they are far from exhaustive. Be this as it may, they are grouped in four sections dealing sequentially with management, regulation, supervision and resolution.

First and foremost, let me emphasize four major findings that are axiomatic to me and will permeate the whole of this chapter.

Firstly, excess liquidity blurs both bankers' and supervisors' sense of risk, and it can be a forerunner of insolvency.

This article adds new lessons learned by the author to those discussed in the preceding chapters of this book. It also brings together, structures and expands on them, with the benefit of hindsight. Written in January 2017, a summary appeared in the Spanish newspaper *El País* on 12 March 2017.

© The Author(s) 2019
A. de Juan, *From Good to Bad Bankers*,
https://doi.org/10.1007/978-3-030-11551-7_12

Secondly, if a bank is sound its books will be transparent, but if it is in trouble problems will be swept under the carpet.

Thirdly, 'black holes' cannot be filled by accounting tricks, but only with real money.

Fourthly, when things go wrong, relying on time or hypothetical growth rather than corrective action will only make things worse.

2   Management

1. Poor management and ineffective supervision often trigger bank failures and may outweigh macro factors as causal or aggravating conditions.

2. Bad management and weak supervision are closely bound up together. Irrespective of the macro context, when supervision is lenient, good bankers may tend to become bad in a behavioural process that typically develops over four sequential stages:

First stage: incompetence. While there may be other causes, current losses and undercapitalization or insolvency generally appear as a result of rapid growth and poor lending. Indeed, excess liquidity all too often leads to runaway expansion, both major causes of crisis.

Other than excess liquidity, the concentration of risk in specific borrowers or groups of borrowers, industries or products is likely to prove fatal over time. Real estate, mortgages and 'toxic' financial products are the quintessential examples from the current crisis. The concentration of risks in related-party loans is particularly malign.

The mismatch of terms between assets and liabilities (whether as agreed originally with borrowers or induced by default or refinancing arrangements) may lead to an escalation of serious liquidity problems. Interest rate and foreign exchange mismatch are also to be blamed.

Extravagant expenditure is often a giveaway for poor management and a symptom that applies to other areas.

Second stage: cosmetics. The 'bad banker' spiral appears. Many bankers in trouble refuse to address their problems while they are still manageable. They prefer to sweep them under the carpet, using cosmetic accounting to buy time and retain economic control and social influence.

Third stage: desperate measures or *la fuite en avant*. By definition, cosmetic accounting can never actually solve problems, and as an organization's difficulties mount, the bad banker will be tempted to hazard all on high-risk borrowers and speculation, which only escalates losses and undermines good professional practice.

Contrary to the principles of conventional economics, meanwhile, high risk is not necessarily offset by high interest rates. Rather, the high-risk lender will often fail to collect any interest and may even lose the principal loaned. A friend of mine says that what matters is not the notional return *on* assets, but the actual return *of* assets.

Fourth stage: malpractice. When disaster looms, bad bankers all too often resort to malpractice, which may take a variety of forms, most of them involving related-party lending and even 'self-lending'. In a nutshell, bad bankers tend to siphon money out of their institutions in situations of stress, rather than injecting fresh resources. 'This is legitimate. It's the Government's fault, not mine. It's my children's bread and butter.' So runs the common refrain.

3. The problem is that insolvency often takes root unnoticed in periods of prosperity. Nobody dares 'rain on the parade', not even supervisors. Even if it is a house of cards, a growing economy that generates lots of jobs and burgeoning tax receipts is very attractive for governments of all shades, whatever the risk and future cost. *Après moi, le déluge*. Problems remain hidden in the books. Meanwhile, cronyism between politicians, bankers and borrowers may also play their part.

4. How is this possible? In general, it is done by exploiting the gaps and ambiguities in prudential regulation, and by flawed compliance, abetted by ineffective or overly amicable supervision. As the saying goes, 'there is more than one way to skin a cat', but the main cosmetic technique is to 'refinance' irrecoverable loans, which can be done in many ways. Refinancing good loans in the realistic hope of recovery may be normal practice, but the widespread habit of 'evergreening' bad ones certainly is not. It prevents transparency and is a serious obstacle to supervision. Refinancing bad loans and other cosmetic practices result in the paradox that the worst loans (in terms of risk and size) are not recognized as past due or impaired in the books. This offers an important lesson: since the recognition of 'arrears' in the accounts is often an optimistic and meaningless minimum, supervisors should look not at bad assets, as recognized in the books when examining a bank, but at 'good' ones. The loans which are booked as bad tend to be smaller and will any way already be in the hands of the legal department.

5. The worst transactions, however, are all too often carefully disguised. As the late Bill Taylor of the US Federal Reserve once put it, 'the larger a bank is, the more difficult it will be to manage, control and supervise'. In this light, supervisors could usefully be urged to carefully look at 'good' banks, rather than insisting on those already identified as problematic.

6. Where cosmetic practices prevail, the worst assets are generally under-provisioned or are not provisioned at all. Meanwhile, unrecoverable accruals

tend to be recognized as income, even where they are financed by the lender itself, and the fictitious nature and negative impact of such revenues on cash flows are conveniently ignored. The consequences are grave:

- A part of the earnings, provisions, reserves and equity reflected in a problem bank's books will also be fictitious. However, taxes, dividends and indeed bonuses continue to be paid, escalating losses and eating up liquidity. This only compounds the effects of ongoing bad management and adds to the continuous burden of financing the stock of non-performing assets.
- No corrective action is taken by management either at the board or executive level. Or indeed by supervisors.

7. In such a context, insolvency can grow unnoticed like a cancer, while the banks concerned continue to enjoy easy access to funds in the market, taking new deposits and borrowing on the strength of bogus accounts and the high remuneration of those resources. Wrongly enough, long-term assistance from governments and international institutions may also make life comfortable, allowing management to disregard insolvency and discouraging adjustment. As a result, the true situation is not revealed, as a rule, until banks become illiquid or supervision suddenly becomes more stringent. Until such a time, bad managers, auditors and supervisors often prefer to turn a blind eye, applying a lax interpretation of accounting and prudential rules.

As a rule of thumb, then, we may infer that when a bank needs growing liquidity assistance for a few months, it will probably have undisclosed insolvency problems and its difficulties are all too likely to grow.

8. Let us now return to the matter of asset valuation with a warning against forbearance: it is safer for bankers and supervisors to overestimate than to underestimate losses. Experience tells us that losses in difficult times will always prove deeper than initially admitted by managers, auditors and even the toughest supervisor. It is human nature. Provisions are inimical to dividends and bonuses. Consequently, the beneficiaries of such distributions are often keen to avoid setting aside any more than they must.

9. The history of financial crises shows that there are five different levels of estimated losses. Each level sequentially multiplies the previous one by two (or almost by two) in the following rough pattern:

- First, the banker does not recognize any losses at all or, at best, recognizes losses amounting to, say, half of capital.
- The external auditor then steps in and may dare to report that losses are actually twice as deep as the bank's estimates.

- Official bank examiners then examine the bank and once again double the auditor's estimate of losses, often triggering tough corrective action and/or intervention.
- The bank is then placed under public administration or nationalized, and government appointed administrators and controllers, now working from inside the institution, double the losses found by the bank examiners yet again.
- Finally, when the ailing bank is put up for sale, the potential buyer's due diligence procedures find that actual losses were twice as big again, as even the government's administrators were willing to admit. Although it is not unknown for buyers to overstate their case as a form of insurance against unpleasant surprises, buyers are not usually far wrong in their assessments overall.

10. As I have already suggested, all these things happen for lack of firm government control, whether in the regulatory and supervisory field and/or when it comes to resolution:

- Good regulation is necessary, but it is useless without proper supervision
- So good supervision is also necessary. However, neither regulation nor supervision can really help without sound resolution mechanisms.
- So good resolution mechanisms are also necessary, but however sound the mechanisms may be, they will prove futile if regulation and supervision are weak. Furthermore, weak or defective resolution mechanisms, or simply an unwillingness to bring matters to a head, can also thwart even the best supervision.

Regulation, supervision and resolution thus form an interlocking package that cannot be applied piecemeal. In the end, it is a vicious circle. If only one or two components are in place, implementing the third is likely to prove ineffective and a waste of effort. The system could be likened to a chain—it is only as strong as its weakest link.

3   Prudential Regulation

11. Practically all regulators worldwide now seem focused on regulatory capital, an obvious supervisory approach

However, asset valuation and mandatory provisions for arrears and impairments are only weakly regulated in most countries. Proper income recognition may not even be regulated. As a result, regulatory capital per books, however defined, often proves an ineffective guide, and it is in any case not necessarily real capital. Let us remind ourselves that cosmetic practices will take hold in problem banks if it is left to each individual bank to measure its own assets or set its own models for capital requirements without proper supervision. Hence, shortfalls in provisions as well as reserves based on fictitious income should be deducted from equity per books to identify the real level of own resources.

12. In this connection, let me emphasize here that International Accounting Standard 39, which has been in force for the last decade, has in practice degraded the traditional principle of prudence, that pillar of transparent accounting according to which foreseeable problems should immediately be recognized, but anticipated economic benefits should not be booked until they materialize. As a result, bad loans are now recognized only when they are legally in arrears or when a loss is actually incurred, rather than when merely expected, for lack of repayment capacity of the borrower. Transparency has given way to opacity. This serious problem is now supposed to be addressed by new international regulations (signally International Financial Reporting System (IFRS) 9). Even so, the treatment of expected losses which should be based on the repayment capacity of the borrower remains rather lax and the standard will anyway not enter into force until 2018. Other than that, proper regulation of unrecoverable accruals remains in the limbo of irrelevance.

13. As regards income recognition, we may note that specific provisions have now become somewhat unfashionable among many regulators, and are being replaced by capital requirements and general provisions. Of course, I have no objection to such arrangements so long as they are realistic. Yet both focus by nature on blocks of potentially impaired assets but fail to identify the specific borrowers who are in trouble, and neither can stop the fictitious recognition of unrecoverable accruals as income in the books. Hence, these mechanisms cast a deep shadow over transparency, however much they may reinforce banks' solvency as a whole, because they sidestep the timely suspension of interest, perhaps the most important prudential tool in the supervisory armoury, as an early warning that stops hidden losses from snowballing. Income on paper is mistaken for actual cash flows, the only element that really counts in economic terms.

14. Moreover, various components of regulatory capital go beyond substantial, ordinary equity items (i.e. paid-in capital and retained earnings) to include a number of low-quality items. All in all, then, capital requirements as a whole can be fairly lenient and may fail to fulfil their expected role.

Let us consider just some low-quality components:

- In my opinion, convertible securities, such as the so-called CoCos (contingent convertible bonds) should not be considered as real capital, because until they are converted into capital or written off, they are just another liability. Besides, they are a very expensive form of borrowing and, as such, they hurt banks' profitability. Also, they do not provide any fresh cash when they are converted, which is crucial in cases of resolution. Rather, liquidity was injected in the past, at the time securities of this kind were subscribed.
- Deferred tax assets are not real capital, even if guaranteed by government. They are just an expectation of future tax exemptions in the event of potential profits. Other than that, they contain no liquidity.
- Goodwill or bad will (i.e. the positive or negative difference between the price paid in an acquisition and the book value) is just an accounting entry and certainly not capital. The price paid is precisely the market value of the asset acquired.
- Conceptually worse, capital is often considered as coverage for expected losses, where it should be considered only as a potential coverage for unexpected ones. Expected losses should be charged as provisions against the profit and loss account. Otherwise, capital per books will be fictitious to the extent of unprovisioned losses.

15. Capital regulations do not always capture the risk involved in some areas, rendering them partly meaningless. Key concerns of this kind would include:

- concentration of risk in specific borrowers, groups of borrowers or industries;
- real consolidation perimeters, including consolidation of off-shore vehicles and affiliated undertakings which are less than 50% owned by the institution supervised but are nonetheless under the parent's actual control;
- risk inherent in some off-balance sheet items, including derivatives and special products; and
- potential inconsistency between the accounting and prudential standards applied in consolidated subsidiaries abroad and in the parent company.

16. Another key weakness of mandatory capital ratios derives from the concept of risk-weighted supervision (RWS), which has now been adopted worldwide and bases capital requirements on 'risk-weighted assets' (RWA). The risk approach does indeed make sense, but it has serious side effects and is not necessarily reliable. Why? Because

- risk assessment is based on past information, if and when available, but the future is difficult to capture in these terms;
- bad bankers can easily manipulate the risk inherent in each type of asset to bring it into line with the desired capital level;
- the stress on RWA induces bankers to sacrifice lending in favour of assets with a lower or even zero weighting, such as sovereign debt, often in undesirable proportions. As if sovereign debt were always risk-free; and
- weightings differ from country to country, hindering international comparison.

17. In this light, an effective and rigorous leverage ratio is needed, either alongside or instead of the RWA measure. Such a ratio could prevent risk manipulation by comparing capital with total assets, which is an objective figure. Sadly, the current 3% established by Basel III looks overly lenient as a standard. In fact, banks with strict leverage ratios in countries like the US suffered much less in the recent crisis than those relying on other ratios. The suggestion is that if risk-based capital requirements are also maintained, then the level of capital required should be the higher of the two ratios.

18. Since investment banking activities and financial engineering were at the root of the recent financial crisis, the Volker, Vickers and Liikanen initiatives, not to mention the Dodd-Frank Act, all aimed in their different ways to address these problems. However, they were watered down, probably at the behest of bankers' lobbies, and their outcomes leave something to be desired. A good example is the separation of commercial from investment banking, which proved somewhat less than strict.

Bankers constantly harp on the theme that regulations are too complex, changeable and suffocating, providing an incentive only to relocate to more accommodating jurisdictions or switch to less tightly regulated financial activities. Self-serving though these claims may be, they nevertheless deserve some attention insofar as they may also contain a grain of truth and, in fact, dislocation may actually happen. Regulations should be tough and simple. Yet they should also be realistic and permanent.

4   Supervision

19. Since macro factors do trigger systemic crises, macroprudential supervision is a must. Other than just an internationally agreed concept, however, macroprudential supervision should be institutionalized and closely coordinated with micro supervision. Indeed, they should operate under a strong,

common authority, particularly bearing in mind that 'intellectuals' (macro) and 'policemen' (micro) make uneasy bedfellows.

20. Tough supervision can help plug regulatory gaps, but weak oversight can undermine even the soundest of regulations. The experiential evidence is overwhelming: supervision is more important than regulation. In this connection, let us recall a basic principle:

In times of prosperity and easy liquidity, supervision easily becomes increasingly tolerant, so that benevolent diagnoses, eyebrow-raising and verbal recommendations take the place of cease and desist orders, intervention and resolution. Life looks rosy, and both bankers and supervisors are happy. Anything goes. This leaves room for nasty surprises, however. So, against those who advocate limited supervision for reasons of cost, it should be emphasized that there is no costlier arrangement than poor supervision or no supervision at all.

21. The problem today is that on-site verification of credit files, which remains the most effective form of supervision, is being side-lined and diluted in practice worldwide, having wrongly come to be seen as an overwhelming or intrusive task that is almost impossible to perform and that 'belongs to the stone age'.

As a result, supervisors tend to disregard two very effective tools:

(a) Proper use of sampling techniques to verify the real repayment capacity of a borrower on site, irrespective of whether the loan concerned is formally past due or not.
(b) On-site verification of loans to confirm that debts are serviced out of real cash flows generated by the borrower. Even where verification procedures survive, inspection procedures are often subject to strict time constraints and quantified adjustments are all too often brushed aside.

22. On-site identification of potential losses is, then, being replaced by fancier, more 'scientific' but less demanding and effective mechanisms. These may have failed so far, but they put less pressure on supervisors. This has been particularly the case with external auditing, mathematical models and stress tests. These tools are no doubt useful supplements to on-site supervision, but they can also prove superficial or misleading and should never replace it. Their dismal record in the recent financial crisis and even currently is notorious, the main reason for this failure being supervisory forbearance or unreliable information supplied by problem banks.

Additionally, much emphasis has been placed more recently on procedure reviews and strengthening good governance as supervisory tools. Though useful enough in themselves, these tools are now all too often regarded as a panacea to supplant verification and quantification. This is a mistake that leads to lax surveillance of asset quality, which is key to preventing insolvency.

23. External auditing is itself a tricky area that deserves some special comments.

Theoretically, the statutory role of auditors differs from and supplements that of supervisors. This is the main line of defence of auditors when they are criticized for inaccuracy or mistakes. However, auditors and supervisors should always work hand in hand, particularly in times of crisis, under the guiding principle that 'four eyes see better than two'. In any event, unless given specific and focused terms of reference by the supervisor, auditors should not be used by supervisors in place of bank examiners, as their findings may prove fluid on matters of decapitalization and adjustments.

Let us remind ourselves that auditors are responsible to the client institution's stakeholders. In this context, some auditors do sterling work. Congratulations!

But others do not. Still, public criticism of audit failures is rather subdued. Let us see some typical scenarios:

- When supervisors are easy-going, some auditors follow their lead and issue more lenient reports, further masking transparency. 'We cannot be tougher than the supervisor', they seem to think.
- Even if supervisors are strict and actively seek to air existing problems, some auditors may yet be sensitive to pressure and moderate their opinions in their clients' reports.

In both cases, bad bankers sometimes brandish auditors' reports against the supervisory authorities, in the media and even in court.

24. Independence and transparency are key to a sound audit industry. However, dependent relations may develop where a firm audits the same institutions for long periods of time or does significant consultancy work for audit clients.

No matter how influential their lobbies may be, the external auditors' charter needs to redefine their typical functions and should be tightened up so as to prevent the problems mentioned.

Here are some suggestions:

— Future regulations could require auditors formally to state in their reports whether or not they received all necessary information from the audited institution to reach reliable conclusions.
— Another possibility would be to have supervisors engage auditors directly and have them work under specific terms of reference. The supervisor would pay the auditors for their work and then charge the cost on to the institution examined.
— Finally, rotation requirements could be revisited to enhance independence, perhaps by legislating mandatory periodic changes in the audit provider instead of a mere switch between partners of the same firm, or by periodically excluding incumbents from auditor selection processes.

25. *Mathematical modelling* has proved a failure in most cases thus far. Contrary to their original objectives, the Basel II models in fact lowered banks' capital requirements to insignificant levels and failed to improve bankers' sense of risk. One need only recall what happened in the recent crisis. Why? Because of the following:

— Bad bankers, and even some good ones, may tailor their models to reduce their capital requirements, or manipulate them after they have been built. Yet even the recent international regulations expect models to be built 'internally' by the banks themselves, despite the unreliability of the information provided by problem institutions. Let me insist: when a bank is prosperous it will be transparent, and when it is not, problems will be concealed.
— Models are built by mathematicians and often lack professional inputs from highly skilled, experienced bankers.
— Boards, and even supervisors, do not necessarily understand the models used.
— In any event, models estimate risk as a statistical probability that can be measured, but they are inherently unable to capture what Andrew Sheng (to my mind the leading international expert in financial supervision) calls 'unknown unknowns', which is to say radical uncertainty. Let us think of upheavals such as the black swan liquidity crisis of 2007, the collapse of Lehman Brothers in 2008, the sovereign debt crisis triggered in 2010, the pro-Brexit vote in the UK's recent referendum or the recent Deutsche Bank problems.

26. Many now claim that stress tests are the future. But they too proved a failure in some signal cases in the recent crisis, and their performance has scarcely improved to date.

If they had, how could you explain the sudden unveiling of deep insolvency in relevant banks in Germany, Italy, Portugal and Spain without timely red flags or effective corrective action? Some experts joke that 'Stress tests are aimed at removing stress from supervisors'.

There is nothing like a realistic base scenario, but even those used to build the models used in stress testing are open to question when they rely on unverified data, and all the more so in adverse conditions.

27. Supervision of procedures is, of course, praiseworthy. But it often becomes a cumbersome bureaucratic exercise and, as such, it cannot replace on-site verification of asset values and performance.

28. Measures to bolster governance are also praiseworthy, but governance is very difficult to control and requires a serious compliance culture, which may be conspicuous by its absence. Moreover, codes are often flouted. We see relevant examples every day, including major decisions taken outside of board and executive committee meetings, or without proper debate at these levels. A clear example is the long list of relevant international banks that have recently been fined for malpractice Finally, one might ask as an acid test how stronger governance can be seen as a 'magic bullet' for effective oversight when supervisors seem to live quite happily with outrageous remuneration policies and a general lack of management transparency, both quintessential features of bad governance?

Meanwhile, Basel IV plans to compute legal or regulatory impropriety as one of the elements requiring higher capital levels. The problem, however, is that this approach will probably be based on past penalties, which do not necessarily determine future behaviour.

So, strengthening governance and supervising conduct are welcome concepts but ineffective tools in the short run. And they certainly should not replace verification.

29. It might still be argued that supervisors must be flexible. Very well, but just how flexible? Some degree of flexibility or forbearance might prove wise where external conditions or the situation of a target institution are clearly and steadily improving. In the face of ongoing deterioration, however, forbearance is tantamount to suicide, relegating the supervisor to the role of paper tiger, just when the threat of enforcement action must be believable for the bad banker. Here are just some of the things that happen when excessive flexibility and forbearance take over as a toothless alternative to proper supervision:

- By definition, delinquent loans and the outstanding stock of unprovisioned losses are non-performing assets. Yet their financing has a real cost and involves real cash outflows. So, the institution's stock of losses and liquidity situation worsen day by day. Merely trusting to time to correct such problems will only make matters worse.
- Failing to address problems allows bad managers to stay at the helm, in all likelihood worsening an already difficult situation.
- A perverse message is sent to the market that the bad banker will never be punished, providing an incentive for malpractice and fraud.
- Worse still, a lax supervisor is likely to become a prisoner of its own mistakes and even a prisoner of the institutions it oversees. As such, the supervisor will be reluctant to contradict itself or change course in the future, and an ailing institution may resort to the argument that its methods were good enough in the past, so why not now.

5   Resolution

30. In most cases, identifying losses is a gradual process, and it takes time. Therefore, even if an institution is not illiquid, decapitalization needs to be addressed as soon as equity is seriously eroded, because insolvency is in most cases already present. Like relying on time, relying on growth as a solution can prove a costly mistake. As a rule, underlying and hidden losses will continue to grow ever faster. Even better management will find it hard to keep up. In other words, the later problems are addressed, the costlier the outcomes.

Meanwhile, both banks and the economy as a whole may enter a vicious circle, in which a dearth of credit and poor allocation of resources inflict further damage and cause growing unemployment, in turn affecting the banks' health and squeezing their willingness and ability to lend.

31. Failure by supervisors to take corrective action because of fiscal or procyclical concerns often proves short-sighted and is likely only to aggravate matters. In fact, the cost of inaction ultimately turns out higher every time and may end up requiring the use of taxpayers' money. Cancer needs treatment, however awkward the moment.

32. The ultimate goal of resolution should be to make systems sustainably robust rather than allowing struggling and zombie banks to stagger on. The objective of government action should therefore be to put problems clearly behind the institutions affected and be able to forget about them. If their efforts are half-hearted, banks will remain vulnerable and the danger of recurrence and systemic contagion will persist. Moreover, it is unfair to provide

direct financial aid while bad bankers are still in place, and it is in any case a waste of money. Two principles should always be observed in this regard:

- A good and sustainable level of tangible ordinary capital and, crucially, earnings must be achieved in terms of real cash flows.
- Owners, boards and managers must be changed at an early stage of treatment.

33. As regards recapitalization, 'black holes' can only be properly plugged with solid, permanent resources supplied in the following order:

- retained earnings generated by real profits rather than plucked from thin air by accounting gimmicks
- asset sales
- capital injections by former owners and/or sound new partners
- subscribers of securities subject to the bail-in principle as described below
- official mechanisms, including taxpayers' money, if need be

34. What about loans and guarantees? These tools can help as long as they add to, rather than replacing, the injection of real capital. Addressing insolvency by the simple expedient of providing liquidity to problem banks over a long period of time is a frequent and grave mistake. Massive lending under whatever guise cannot be conceived as a substitute for financial recapitalization of insolvent banks. Such assistance should not be granted to them. Failed institutions should instead be quickly treated as resolution cases.

What about monetary expansion by central banks? Such policies certainly help to solve systemic emergencies and create an appearance of stability, but only in the short term. Furthermore, they do nothing to cure insolvency as such, because they cannot go on forever. A lifeboat may save the crew from drowning, but it cannot stop the sinking ship from eventually going under. This kind of policy can seriously disrupt banking systems by making it difficult for good banks to obtain reasonable margins. Furthermore, monetary expansion of this kind is likely to create risky bubbles, as well as an atmosphere of moral hazard in which bankers and even supervisors lose their sense of risk and become ever more likely to shy away from painful adjustments and corrective action.

35. *Mergers* are a tempting recipe and, according to some, a miracle cure. Beware! It all depends on the circumstances. Let us consider some of the main problems with this strategy:

- Mergers of two or more ailing banks will only swell their problems.
- Even acquisitions of ailing banks by stronger ones, a favourite resolution mechanism, may complicate matters if the new business is not properly recapitalized and managed.
- Merging large banks can also have serious drawbacks even if the original institutions are healthy, because it can create systemic institutions which are too big—or too interconnected with other banks—to fail or to be resolved. Such institutions are hard to manage, difficult to supervise and practically impossible to resolve. They are doomed to linger indefinitely in the market, like the undead, and they wield great influence over supervisors, whose hands may anyway be tied by the difficulty of taking any drastic measures.

In any kind of mergers, supervisors must keep in mind certain additional risks:

- Merged institutions tend to blur accounts. Some commentators even go so far as to say that this is the true goal of both owners and supervisors.
- They certainly do not always reduce losses by way of synergies. Unless it is clear from the outset which bank has the whip hand, mergers engender power struggles and provide an excuse for enormous increases in executive pay and egregious severance packages for losers.
- Governments and supervisors can find themselves beholden to the entities created by unsuccessful mergers carried out with their blessing, or even at their bidding, so that no further corrective action will ever be taken against them.

36. Burden-sharing is a very sound concept. Shareholders, creditors and the financial services industry should contribute to the recapitalization of banks and rescue of banking systems ahead of the long-suffering taxpayer. Even so, if the industry is systemically vulnerable and/or if supervisors only address insolvency belatedly, when capital has been lost several times over and sizable funds are needed, then taxpayers will eventually have to foot a considerable part of the bill.

37. Let me elaborate on the modern concept of bail-in or burden-sharing through internal recapitalization. This novel idea is perfectly sound inasmuch as it means that the holders of deposits above a given limit and of non-senior securities must contribute to wipe out losses before government steps in. Bail-ins thus reduce, and can even eliminate, the cost of rescue for governments. However, they also have serious drawbacks:

- While it is obvious that shares must be written off, other securities subject to bail-in are not capital but rather very expensive liabilities and an obstacle to profitability until they are converted into capital or written off.
- Bail-in operations may provide capital when it is needed, but they do not inject liquidity, which is also needed for effective resolution. This is because liquidity is obtained only when securities are issued, but no new money is likely to be forthcoming while resolution is under way.
- The risk inherent in products like deposits and certain types of debt securities can be extremely difficult for individual investors to assess, which raises marketing and moral issues, not to mention legal ones. Therefore, such instruments should preferably be sold to institutional investors only, following adequate disclosure of the fine print of contracts and the financial health of the issuer.
- In any event, the effect of bail-ins on markets may prove an inhibiting factor for potential investors. The full extent of this side effect remains to be seen, however.

38. Another classic bank recapitalization tool is to set up 'bad banks' by carving out bad assets and removing their management from the ailing institution. However, this only works under certain strict conditions:

- The bad bank is structured as a standalone entity, free of any remaining legal, financial, managerial or de facto ties with the problem bank from which the bad assets are to be carved out. Meanwhile, managers should scrupulously avoid artificial structures and supervisors should immediately strike down any that may be proposed. Deconsolidation is a must. Otherwise, there will be no real clean up, no matter how imaginative the legal architecture may be. It is like moving rubbish from one room to another of the same house.
- While bad banks may have to be at least partly government owned, as the lesser of two evils, they should preferably be private institutions owned by the financial industry. On occasion, they may also have to be partly financed or backed by additional government loans and guarantees. Bad banks should only acquire assets from ailing banks once new owners (whether buyers, strategic partners or governments) have replaced those who caused or presided over their failure.
- A bad bank should only buy bad assets, and priority should be given to the worst, so that losses are actually cleaned. Buying good assets will only inject liquidity into the problem bank, but it will not help it start afresh.

– Asset pricing is key to effective clean-up operations by bad banks. The basic principle is that losses do not disappear, and someone always foots the bill. Let us consider the three options available:

- Net book value. The loss embedded in the bad assets is entirely cleaned up in the ailing bank and is absorbed by the bad bank, which will pick up the tab whether it is owned by the government, the financial services industry or both.
- Market value. The loss remains in the ailing bank, which must immediately be recapitalized via the resolution mechanisms in place. This is the only case in which the eventual liquidation of the assets acquired by the bad bank can reasonably be expected to generate a profit for the buyer over time.
- Compromise price lying somewhere between net book value and market value. This means that the 'bad bank' must absorb part of the losses down to the level of market value, while the losses remaining in the ailing bank will have to be absorbed by some other contributor depending on the resolution mechanism adopted.

39. *The other pillar of resolution is change of ownership and management.* In other words, the decks must be cleared. This must be thorough and quick, and it must be completed before any official financial assistance is provided. Otherwise, any aid granted will benefit the previous bankers, as we have seen in a number of international cases, where 'rescue finance' was used to pay, and even increase, severance packages, emoluments, bonuses and/or dividends. As a rule, banking systems have to be saved in order to protect depositors and employees, and to safeguard payment systems. However, bankers themselves should not be shielded in any way from the effects of their decisions. Such an outcome is outrageous, unfair and grossly ineffective. Besides, it only encourages professional malpractice and egregious risk-taking.

When it comes to replacing existing directors and managers, let me emphasize that it is crucial to choose the right staff to take charge of an ailing bank. Proper management of such banks demands a very special combination of executive expertise and attitude. To fight a war, you need a general; to remove a cancer, you need a surgeon. Meanwhile, any managerial staff who may stays on and all new managers should be subjected to proper screening. Otherwise, they may yet spring a few surprises of their own.

40. Whenever fraud of any kind is discovered, legal action should be energetically pursued against former directors and managers, in addition to or instead of any civil liability incumbent on the problem institution. Impunity

must not prevail, and specific cases of fraud should be taken to court. Apart from restitution for injured parties, this provides a strong deterrent against moral hazard in the system.

41. Governments may sometimes have to step in as temporary owner or manager of an ailing bank, where this is unavoidable, to pave the way for a final change of ownership. The key principles in this regard are as follows:

- To the extent it means a kind of nationalization, government should stay only for a brief period before returning the institution to the market. One or two years would be a reasonable deadline.
- Government should preferably be replaced by large, financially strong owners or strategic partners able to ensure a robust and sustainable future. Proper screening also applies to owners.
- A problem bank could also be offered to the market by way of one or more capital issues over a longer period, while remaining under government control. However, this course should be taken only after a bank's capital and earnings have been fully rebuilt and a strong and stable management team has taken the reins.

42. Governments and supervisors should avoid any premature victory lap before it is certain that all problems have been fully resolved. Such claims cheat the market and those who make them risk falling prisoner to their own boasts, so that their hands are tied when fresh difficulties emerge.

43. Dealing with insolvent banks is a dirty business. Conflict is inevitable, whether with former owners and investors, unseated managers, borrowers, staff, unions, tax payers, or politicians and their cronies. Dirty as it may be, however, such work is preferable to the alternatives.

44. I would like to conclude by stressing the importance of realism. Airline pilots like to say that any landing is a good landing, which needs no further gloss or explanation. We might paraphrase this maxim in the case of bank resolution by saying, 'Any loss is a good loss, as long as it is the last'.

45. I still have one final reflexion, what the French would call *la réflexion de l'escalier*; that is to say, something you realize you should have said only after leaving a meeting or discussion. Against the approach I have taken in this chapter, some might say, 'This is all well and good, but if you find yourself in a context of serious economic and political uncertainty, perhaps priority should be given to stability rather than vigorous supervision.' Who knows if this reflection is not even now driving policy in any number of countries?

On the face of it, it sounds sensible. Even so, governments should be aware that such hands-off stability may well prove shallow and ephemeral. If so, a deeper crisis may soon erupt at a much higher cost in terms of economic, social and political repercussions. Those who fail to address problems when their systems are in trouble will also eventually suffer in one way or another.

13

Non-performing Loans: NPLs

Ten years after the crisis began, numerous European banks still hold significant volumes of non-performing assets on their balance sheets, generating further losses on a daily basis. However, many of them paradoxically report high levels of equity. What is going on here?
A. de Juan

1 Supervision

1.1 Home Truths on Europe's NPLs

Europe needs to overcome fears of a hypothetical crisis and impose more intrusive supervision and greater provisioning on its banks.

The issue of non-performing loans (NPLs) in Europe is now receiving the policy attention it deserves albeit some ten years since the start of the global financial crisis. Of course, many regulatory efforts during these years are praiseworthy. But it is worrying that NPLs are still a serious problem in a large number of significant banks in Europe, especially as many of these banks show a satisfactory level of regulatory capital in their books. Rather than just looking at bank problems with a forward-looking approach, it is vital to focus on the present as a priority.

Paper presented by the author at the Second Annual Conference of the European Systemic Risk Board (ESRB), chaired by Mario Draghi, which was held in Frankfurt on 22 September 2017. Later published by the *Central Banking Journal*.

2   Questionable Impressions

A relevant—but often disregarded—fact about the unprovisioned part of non-performing assets is that they do not generate any yield, while the liabilities that support those assets carry real costs and act as a cash drain. This creates current losses and a worsening of liquidity. Continuously.

While it is good that international regulators have focused strongly on boosting bank capital, less attention has been paid to supervision, asset valuation and provisioning, which could prevent or reduce the number and size of crises, including their effective solutions. An analogy would be the focus on paying for a funeral rather than preventing the need for one in the first place.

Building up a common regulatory framework and supervisory practice in Europe is a very difficult and lengthy task. But one cannot avoid the impression that strict regulation and supervision have been softened by the European authorities for the sake of the hypothetical stability of the financial system or the economy.

The dream of a hypothetical 'beautiful normality' is an ideal. It is even possible that monetary expansion would help to achieve this normality in the short term. But the future may prove to be neither beautiful nor normal. Such a policy would be tantamount to thinking: 'We do mean to improve things, but … not yet'

In fact, the current stability appears to be very vulnerable on a number of strategic fronts, including the pending problem of systemic NPLs and serious geopolitical instability.

There is excess liquidity, which make bankers lose their sense of risk and leads to bubbles, as debt grows due to lower yields. Additionally, there is president Donald Trump's threat of US deregulation, which may prove contagious in Europe and elsewhere. These issues should be ringing alarm bells because of their similarities with the lead-up to 2007.

What is needed, therefore, is to address the problems of the financial system head on, thoroughly and gradually as they appear, without being afraid of potential consequences. Otherwise, sitting on the fence may lead to a more serious crisis—and sooner, rather than later.

3   Oft-disregarded 'Rules of Thumb'

There are a number of practical reminders that some financial supervisors disregard at their peril. First, problem banks almost always systematically hide their problem assets, thereby leading to unreliable information on their books. Consequently, any regulation on capital or asset quality is most likely to be ineffective or misleading, if based on 'unverified' information provided by the banks.

Unverified information based on off-site analyses, audits, reports, models, stress tests, risk-weighted asset valuation, and even compliance with capital requirements, may also prove to be unreliable.

Second, the worst loans by size and risks are never recorded as 'past due'. Instead, they are most often disguised as good loans, through loan restructuring. As a result, one is not able to uncover the hidden losses because the financial position and capital on the books will be fictitious.

That is why the key to prudential supervision is reliable asset evaluation through on-site inspections. In my experience, for asset evaluations to be realistic, they should be verified by on-site, case-by-case inspection, aimed at recording the market value of foreclosures and the estimated value of loans based on the borrowers' repayment capacity. This should be undertaken over and above the formal reporting of loan arrears or 'incurred arrears', which can be easily manipulated.

Third, the specific level of provisions, as well as the suspension of unpaid interest as income, should be imposed promptly, despite management resistance. Provisions and accrual suspensions are the enemy of dividends, emoluments and bonuses for top management—important factors that explain why bankers avoid provisions.

In other words, the timely imposition by supervisors of proper provisioning and suspension on unpaid interest as income (on a case-by-case basis) is the most effective preventive measure to stop the snowballing of hidden NPL losses. Gradual but disciplined remedial action by management and supervisors when problems are identified (rather than accumulating hidden losses) will prove very effective and will reduce the number and depth of crises.

The blame of unaddressed NPLs can be squarely laid at the door of management, which is primarily responsible to shareholders and to the market. However, it takes real political will to censure regulators and supervisors in any way.

Fourth, we need to say upfront that capital as per books is not real capital. Real capital is capital as per books, minus the shortfall in pending provisions on NPLs and recorded reserves that were retained from fictitious income.

We should be honest that real capital is also affected by the poor quality of some of the components of regulatory capital. These include 'CoCos'—contingent, convertible capital instruments—that are liabilities as long as the issuer does not fail. CoCos are also a very expensive liability that constitutes an incentive for high-risk lending in times when return on assets is stagnating. Items such as goodwill and deferred tax assets are also questionably allowable as bank capital, since they have little loss-absorption capacity.

Bluntly speaking, real capital should be in place to cover future 'unknown unknowns'. If new capital is used to cover current losses, we may welcome the liquidity injection, but it is not real regulatory capital. Regulatory capital should be 'clean' capital available to meet all future losses.

One last observation on capital is that issuing new capital when a bank has negative net worth without making the situation transparent to potential subscribers is a deceitful malpractice. Remember the famous principle: 'Do not throw good money after bad.'

Fifth, the current focus on a forward-looking approach to supervision is no substitute for quality on-site supervision that focuses on the present.

Sixth, we should welcome the continuing efforts to strengthen bank governance as a supervisory tool. However, this is not a substitute for inspection because sound governance is a long-term objective that is fluid, and difficult to control and manage. Cultural change only happens gradually, and can only be achieved in the long term.

This underlines the fact that regulatory forbearance—particularly the tolerance of lax practices in asset valuation or cosmetic accounting—is the enemy of transparency, and can hardly coexist with good bank governance.

Seventh, the practice of liquidity support as a supervisory tool. Bank deposit runs may appear suddenly, caused by panic from lack of confidence or a one-off event, they add to the lack of self-generated cash-flows due to the decapitalization of banks. Supervisors step in at that point, not before—at a time when intervention is both too late and too expensive.

Traditionally, liquidity support or lender-of-last-resort facilities are short-term and at high cost, as an incentive for bank managers and supervisors to take quick corrective action. However, treating decapitalization or insolvency just with liquidity support in whatever modality will not 'refill the hole' of capital inadequacy or insolvency.

On the contrary, prolonged and massive central bank liquidity support at low or zero interest rates, are 'false friends'. Irrespective of the objective of inflation targeting, economic recovery or improving non-recurrent bank profits, monetary expansion may prove effective for a while, but if perpetuated, they carry serious risks. For example, they will result in changes in banking business models, stagnation of return on assets, bubbles and moral hazard that leads to excessive bank lending and risk-taking.

The conclusion is that any financial engineering mechanism, including the creation of 'bad bank resolution schemes', should be avoided if it favours the bankers who caused or presided over the problems, if it involves cosmetics to show a healthy picture to the market or if it bets on unrealistic recovery of the price of bad assets. Such financial engineering creates expectations that may not materialize because the lack of performance of non-performing assets, as well as maintenance, marketing and servicing costs, can lead to bad outcomes for the financial engineering scheme.

For 'bad bank' resolution schemes to be effective, they should buy bad assets at market prices. Needless to say, any unprovisioned losses will materialize at the point of transfer to the 'cleaned-up bank' and should be automatically charged to reserves. If the prices of bad assets are set above market prices, the losses will be embedded in the bad bank, and will have to be properly and promptly covered by the rescue package.

4 Mechanism for NPL Resolution

Finally, in addition to the bad bank resolution mechanism, one cannot exclude other mechanisms for solving the non-performing asset or NPL problem. However, a number of mechanisms currently in place have proved artificial and ineffective.

Why have NPLs and non-performing assets not been liquidated, remaining as burdens to a number of European banks and countries? Most of the time, it is because they are not properly provisioned, and their sale would materialize or crystallize the losses.

It is true that this situation persists because excess liquidity in the market also discourages liquidation. But at the right price, there is always a market.

Consequently, the best way to promote prompt liquidation of NPLs and other non-performing assets is to have them valued in the books at recovery value or market price respectively. In this way, their sale will not materialize any new losses.

5 Tightening the Screw

For many people, International Financial Reporting Standard 9 represents great progress, and they feel there is no need for more tightening of regulation and supervision. I do not share that view because the new panacea, the concept of 'expected losses' (evolved after the inertia of more than a decade of emphasis on 'incurred losses'), is qualified by numerous caveats that may be subject to restrictive interpretation. Furthermore, it expected losses are based on 'internal' mathematical models and the new regulation wrongly maintains income recognition in respect of unpaid interest, which is one of the worst enemies of financial supervision.

Many experts think that progress will be limited, especially when applied to problem banks. The tightening of the screw should be applied to a stricter treatment of expected losses and to supervisory practices. In my view, new standards for financial reporting should be issued.

As part of that tightening, regulations on non-performing assets should make it mandatory for them to be booked at market value. In other words, they should be properly provisioned as soon as a potential loss is identified. If things get better, a phase-in period could be established to cushion the impact. It is important to recall that International Financial Reporting Standard 5 established a limit of one year (which was unevenly or poorly applied) to liquidate bad assets. In no case should the deadline exceed a maximum of two years.

Furthermore, unpaid and unpayable accruals should be mandatorily suspended, instead of being recognized as income in the profit-and-loss (P&L) account. The suspension should cover the total principal and not just the non-provisioned part of the loans. The reason is that when a loan is bad, the borrower is not really paying any interest, which is often refinanced by the lender bank itself. This is the classic case of the 'evergreening' of NPLs.

We cannot trust mathematical models that group loans by economic sectors or products, especially if they are used for stress testing. This is even truer if these loan groups are designed by the bad borrower and are not verified and properly quantified.

The required percentage of provisions should be applied over the entire duration of the loan, instead of over a short period or to the discounted present value of the asset. This ensures the books will record the whole loss to be incurred if the asset was liquidated, right from the time the inspection took place.

6   Inspections, Provisions and Capital

The above approach of proper provisioning and suspension of accruals would require a revival of the old supervisory practice of on-site, case-by-case inspection that aims to quantify expected losses. These inspections should last as long as necessary, and should not limit themselves to inspections of banking procedures.

To some, this method of supervision sounds like a return to Stone-Age tools. These inspections were considered cumbersome and time-consuming. However, the intensity of inspections could use traditional sampling mechanisms on the less material assets, saving time and resources. The experience of the US financial crisis and that of other crises have proved that this kind of supervision is more effective than the mechanisms that have been recently put in place.

Indeed, it could be argued that this kind of supervision requires a high number of staff, and is very costly. But history suggests that no supervision or light inspection has proven much costlier at the end of the day. Others have argued that supervisors could be overestimating losses. If that happens, the overestimations from loan recoveries could be credited back to P&L as miscellaneous income. Overall, it is less risky to overestimate losses than to underestimate them.

There is a further argument that covering potential losses with capital (rather than provisions) is safer, as provisions can be manipulated by bad bankers. But this is not necessarily true. Manipulation can be prevented by *ad hoc* supervision, while accounting for capital can also be manipulated. An example is capital based on risk-weighted assets, where risk weightings were often manipulated. One should also bear in mind that some capital subscriptions are partly financed by the issuing institution.

A further argument in favour of specific provisions is the fact that they are more transparent, and would lead to a proper and timely suspension of fictitious accruals. Higher capital cannot do this. In fact, capital cannot be increased every year or easily. Increasing capital at a time of need always proves untimely or too late because the market then begins to suspect the real reasons for capital deficiency.

Indeed, one must underline the fact that if one covers current losses with capital, rather than reducing profits through proper provisioning, one is fostering the bad bankers' moral hazard. Bad bankers will continue to hide losses while paying unjustified taxes and undue dividends, making new bad loans or restructuring them. They will not cut back on management salaries and bonuses. But extravagant expenditure and enhancing bad banking's financial and social influence may continue.

A crucial feature of the proposed mechanism is that when these losses are current, the provision established for losses should be charged immediately to P&L. The surfacing of loan losses allows for the banker's awareness that the bank is deteriorating, but there may still be time for action. This will favour a positive market reaction from management and supervisors to move towards transparency, and then take the necessary corrective actions.

Indeed, gradual and incremental provisioning of losses will prevent big losses appearing suddenly. Loan losses never appear suddenly. Rather, they grow gradually over time. They should, therefore, be captured and treated as soon as they are identified. Proper preventative medicine should always be taken in a timely manner.

Current losses should always be charged to the P&L account. But if losses have accumulated and belatedly unveiled all of a sudden, they should be charged to reserves and capital. This means that if the regulatory capital falls below the prescribed levels, the supervisor can demand immediate recapitalization, giving supervisors the power to prevent further bank deterioration.

To summarize, the ideas aired here will make the liquidation of NPLs and non-performing assets in general easier and more expeditious, when they are booked at market or close to market values. As stated above, there is always a market at the right price. Then, liquidation of bad assets will not trigger any new losses in the books. Instead, the problem bank will finally be cleaned up.

7   Remaining Questions

Timely provisioning over illusory expectations of quick recovery is essential to long-term recovery. Even if timely provisioning would materialize current losses, the bank would become more liquid and return more easily to a normal life.

It is true that this option may unveil the failure of some institutions. The question will then be raised of who should pay the bill, and in what proportions. Shareholders? Creditors? The industry? Or governments?

The unfortunate part of this question is that any other option would face the same problem, whether you use imaginative accounting or unrealistic expectations of quick price recovery. At the end of the day, the hidden 'hole' will surface, and will have to be filled by someone. A hole is a hole, however you describe it. Worse, the hole will prove to be deeper and even worse—the bank in question may become viable, but very vulnerable.

The devil's advocate argument here is: who were the most successful supervisors in getting their systems back to normal and in recovering the funds they put in the rescue operations? Answer: those who acted up front, and injected government and industry money. This was the case in the US. This suggests that recapitalization and resolution rules, which may be still immature, may have to be revisited.

Small pains always avoid larger pains. To paraphrase US general Douglas MacArthur, '[T]he cause of all defeats can be summed up in two words: too late.'

14

Whys and Wherefores of the Spanish Crisis

Lack of experience, political interference, fiscal short-sightedness and lack of political willL lead to inaction or belated and costly action in face of a very deep and widespread financial crisis.
A. de Juan

1   Introduction

The full story of the financial crisis of 2007–2017 is long, bleak and quite possibly unfinished, and it involves a large cast of characters, chief among them the managers and executives responsible for the organizations that failed. However, others also played key roles in Spain, some of whom were decidedly unsuccessful in their actions, including:

– the rating agencies
– property appraisers
– external auditors
– the national regulators and supervisory authorities
– the directors of the new restructuring agency
– the European regulators and supervisory authorities
– certain government ministers

Public paper based on the author's presentation made on 11 December 2017 to the Spanish Parliamentary Committee set up to investigate the recent financial crisis in Spain. The Committee called over 100 key players, witnesses and specialists to present their views. This presentation was considered realistic and unbiased, and was applauded by the deputies of all parties at the end of the session.

© The Author(s) 2019
A. de Juan, *From Good to Bad Bankers*,
https://doi.org/10.1007/978-3-030-11551-7_14

2   The Origins of the International Crisis

The crisis had various causes, and it appeared in different forms in different countries.

In the emblematic case of the US, for example, the financial meltdown affected basically the so-called sub-prime mortgages, which were wrapped up and marketed worldwide using securitization, conduit financing and other instruments in the apogee of financial deregulation.

These sub-prime mortgages granted to poor-quality borrowers were mostly securitized and sold on to funds in the form of bonds, which the banks had no trouble marketing to pension funds, investment funds and so on, in large part thanks to the unduly generous AAA and AA risk ratings blithely handed out by the rating agencies. This mechanism allowed the lender banks to multiply their credit capacity, thereby increasing their profits and further boosting the already stellar earnings of their managers and executives.

Property, and in particular lending to developers, provided the focus for the crisis in Spain. Just before the crisis broke, developers were busily acquiring land in the expectation of obtaining licenses to build new homes, which they expected to sell easily.

This was made possible by wildly generous lending terms offered by the Spanish savings banks and banks, often based on frankly questionable appraisals. Loans were also freely extended to families and individuals, sometimes without any attempt to establish their solvency. Many of these borrowers were not buying a home to live in but as an 'investment', and others even diverted a part of their loans to acquire luxury goods that were entirely unrelated with the properties financed.

At the same time, the savings banks in particular funnelled huge amounts of cash into white elephant projects.

3   The International Bubble

A credit bubble spread to ever more countries in the 1990s, swelling rapidly after the year 2000. This happened in the US after the September 11 terrorist attacks and in Spain after the adoption of the euro as the national currency. However, the bubble did not finally burst until 2007, when a number of German banks and French hedge funds that had purchased bonds used in turn to acquire American sub-prime mortgage securities were found to be in serious difficulties.

This triggered international defaults on a massive scale while illiquidity spread like wildfire, revealing the underlying insolvency of the world's financial systems. However, this was recognized internationally only in September 2008, when the investment bank Lehman Brothers filed for bankruptcy in the US. Contagion appeared immediately elsewhere.

How Did the Bubbles Form? The bubbles arose from a combination of circumstances:

- The end in 1971 of the Bretton Woods systems designed after World War II to prevent any rerun of the financial collapse experienced after the Great Cash of 1929.
- The ideology of financial deregulation extolled by the leading US universities and imposed on governments the world over by international institutions. This dogma demanded blind faith in the market while assuming that banks could look after themselves. Hence, the idea was to avoid any kind of public intervention under the watchword 'No big government'.
- The repeal of legislation adopted in 1933 to prevent retail banks from operating in the capital markets, a business that was reserved for investment banks until the Clinton Administration set aside any restriction in 1999.
- The surplus liquidity sloshing around in the markets as a result of the monetary policies implemented by the world's leading central banks (US Federal Reserve, Bank of Japan and ECB). This upset the balance of payments, among other things allowing surplus German savings to finance the bubble in Spain and other less thrifty European countries. The result was the appearance of negative real interest rates (i.e. nominal interest less inflation), flooding Spanish banks and savings banks with spare cash. Property speculation metastasized nationwide.
- Rapid population growth in Spain following the adoption of the euro. The population swelled by 15% in just seven years from around 40 million people in the year 2000 to 46 million in early 2008. This growth spurt was fed largely by the arrival of immigrants, who needed somewhere to live and so further stimulated the expansion of Spain's housing stock.

These and similar factors drove lending policy out of control in numerous countries, among them Spain, where credit expanded at annual rates of more than 25% as lenders and supervisors alike closed their eyes to this reckless dash down the road to ruin.

4   Why the Savings Banks?

The banking crisis reached Spain in 2007 with the collapse of the European interbank market, which hit the *cajas de ahorro* or savings banks particularly hard because they had based their growth strategy on borrowing in the wholesale markets given the shortage of conventional deposits.

Hence, the crisis in Spain may be put down in large part to bad management and shortcomings in the action of the supervisory authorities.

One singular feature conditioned the whole of the Spanish financial system. In the 1980s, the savings banks had successfully lobbied to be allowed to operate nationwide rather than being restricted to their home regions, which differentiated them from their peers in other European countries. However, their capital was endowed, and they had no shares or equity of any other kind that might have permitted the removal of an institution's managers, enabling a number of grossly incompetent bosses to hang on for years with lamentable results. Furthermore, the failed savings banks had long been prey to political interference, because the new legislation that ushered in their deregulation also reserved some seats on their boards for stakeholder representatives from outside the banking industry. The classic 'fit and proper' condition was in most cases conspicuous by its absence. The importance of this matter only increased in the 1990s, as the savings banks grew in rude health until they accounted for almost 50% of the Spanish financial system.

The intemperate pursuit of interregional growth in Spain and the generalization of incentives and bonuses that rewarded short-term balance sheet growth financed by borrowing in the capital markets were key symptoms of bad management in numerous savings banks, eventually triggering their collapse.

This resulted in a tremendous crisis, and it was the Spanish government that had to foot a considerable part of the bill. Furthermore, the cost of failure was compounded by business closures and rising unemployment, dealing a heavy blow to political stability in Spain.

5   What About the Supervisors?

The vast majority of supervisory authorities worldwide, not to mention their high-powered research departments, were well aware of the economic and financial anomalies affecting the system as a whole, and of the risk of financial bubbles, and Spain was no exception.

Spain already had the legal and regulatory tools needed to contain the bubble. To begin with, the Spanish Bank Discipline and Intervention Act of 1988 placed sufficient coercive powers and tools at the disposal of the supervisor to act in cases of accounting malpractice and fraud, while at the same time providing regulatory tools to bridle imprudent growth in bank balance sheets and to deal with its consequences. For example, these powers allow

- credit restraints to limit the loans to deposits (l/d) ratio;
- limitations on the concentration of risks on a sector-by-sector basis, including the possibility of raising minimum equity requirements and provisions, as in fact happened in the early 1980s;
- limits on the loans to value (l/v) ratio between mortgage loans and the value of mortgaged assets, subject to strict control of appraisals; and
- removal of delinquent or negligent managers, an option that has existed since February 1978.

5.1 The General Failure to React

The supervisory authorities in the countries affected were unwilling to take the necessary measures to burst the bubble or deal with its effects. Nobody wanted to 'stop the party'. The bubble, after all, had considerable positive effects and sparkle in the short term, including:

- dynamic GDP growth
- high tax receipts for governments and town councils
- prosperous construction and ancillary industries
- significant job creation, driving low unemployment
- In Spain, moreover, it was widely held that the so-called statistical provisions required of financial institutions would afford sufficient protection.

Meanwhile, any noxious bubble effects appeared against an international backdrop of surplus liquidity, a shift in ideas about economic cycles and possible government pressure on supervisors to hold back.

5.2 Handling of the Crisis and Roadblocks

The fact is that a grave financial crisis burst upon the world some ten years ago. In Spain, it was seen as the crisis of the savings banks, because their previous vertiginous growth in the property market ended with the failure of no small number of them.

While it is true that the private Spanish banks also engaged in strategies of this kind, they did so to a lesser extent and took on less risk.

Meanwhile, the Spanish authorities' handling of the crisis was tardy, contrived and very costly, much more so, indeed, than it need have been if any sound diagnoses had been made early on and effective measures taken without delay.

It is, of course, true that a number of external roadblocks hindered effective early action, including

- The membership of the savings banks' boards and the absence of ownership rights in the form of shares or other equities. Not a few of their directors, drawn from a wide range of professional fields, were concerned principally to curry favour with the institutions responsible for their appointment in order to ensure their own continuation in office.
- The Bank of Spain sometimes found its supervisory activity hindered by regional governments exercising their devolved powers, particularly in the case of mergers.
- The simplistic application by banks, auditors and supervisors alike of the international accounting standards issued in the early 2000s (in particular IAS 39). By prioritizing actual incurred losses, these new rules pushed the recognition of anticipated losses into the background. To put this another way, the recognition of losses became conditional on the existence of a formal event, like default or a declaration of insolvency, occurring at some time after a loan had been granted. Furthermore, it came to be assumed that all loans, including bad ones, were properly granted, putting off the recognition of losses arising from negligent lending practices.
- The savings banks' inability to issue capital in the form of shares or equivalent securities as a result of their peculiar legal status. They were thus reliant on retained earnings and the issue of hybrid securities to maintain the solvency ratios required by the regulator.
- The very limited number of entities that could potentially acquire the savings banks (which is the normal outcome of a resolution process), and the structural complications inherent in the acquisition of entities that had no shares.

Meanwhile, the supervisory system itself was also beset by its own internal (if soluble) problems:

- Vacillating political will, which was perceived by the markets.
- The erroneous official assumption that property prices would recover in a year or two and that families would always pay their mortgages, so that more forceful measures were considered unnecessary.

- The use of public money came without exception to be considered 'taboo', which proved short-sighted where it was inevitable.
- The authorities' strong aversion to direct intervention and the argument that such hands-on measures created too much noise and projected a negative image. Furthermore, the authorities lacked experience in the management of financial institutions. By closing the door on intervention, this phobia made it nigh on impossible to come clean about an ailing entity's losses, which in turn mediated the supervisory role in relation to verification and transparency.
- The guidelines given to inspectors apparently included advising institutions on how to resolve their regulatory difficulties in formal terms, rather than identifying solvency and management problems and demanding prompt correction.

5.3   First Stage: Confusion, the 'Money Hose' and Regulatory Tolerance

As liquidity dried up internationally in 2007, many became convinced, though their sincerity may in some cases be doubted, that liquidity was at the heart of the matter, when in reality the world faced an insolvency crisis. The talk at the time was all about 'turbulence'. By 2008, however, the funding difficulties encountered by the banks and savings banks had revealed the precariousness of their earnings in prior years, which they had earned by taking on ever more debt and accepting increasingly unmanageable risks. Significantly, the total NPL rate recognized in the Spanish financial system in October 2007 was 0.5% of the total loan portfolio. Naturally, this did not include vast numbers of as yet unrecognized doubtful loans. Four years on, the NPL rate was more than 15%.

As I have said, however, confusion reigned at this point. Governments were inexperienced, and as I have said, the political will was lacking. This remained the case even after the wake-up calls delivered by the collapse of the US investment bank Bear Stearns in March 2008, the scandalous insolvency of the Spanish construction firm Martinsa Fadesa in July and, especially, the failure of Lehman Brothers in September of the same year, though this last event swiftly mobilized resolution mechanisms in many countries. Not so in Spain.

The measures adopted by the Spanish authorities after Lehman's implosion were confined to injecting liquidity into the system by means of what came to be called the manguerazo or 'money hose'. This consisted basically of purchasing good assets from the banks (via the Fondo para la Adquisición de Activos

Financieros (FAAF) programme created ad hoc) and underwriting their securities issues. Also, the standards applicable to the measurement of impairments were relaxed and the provisions required to cover losses were reduced. Refinancing became the chief means of sweeping reality under the carpet.

In early 2009, the Bank of Spain could have cranked up the restructuring mechanisms, which were largely based on the existing deposit guarantee and bad bank mechanisms. These had worked well in the banking crisis of the 1980s and were financed 50/50 by government and the financial system.

This never happened, however, and it was precisely at this time that José Viñals, then vice governor of the Bank of Spain, left to take up a senior post at the IMF and the Spanish finance minister Pedro Solbes was replaced by Elena Salgado.

In fact, 2009 saw a shift towards experimental restructuring formulas. Meanwhile, the government was still obstinately refusing to recognize the delicate condition of the system, as doing so would have given the lie to its protestations that the economy was sound and to its boast that Spain's banking and supervisory systems were perhaps the best in the developed world and a model for others to follow.

As I have already said, the use of public money was seen without exception as taboo, while all means possible were to be used to avoid intervention in ailing institutions. This conditioned the work of the Bank of Spain's inspectorate, and the auditors used at times in their stead were not always up to the task. The practice of refinancing both the principal and interest on bad loans spread. Meanwhile, it became ever more common for institutions to classify problem loans as 'normal' or 'substandard'. Loans classed as normal required no provisions, while substandard loans were not recognized as 'doubtful' in the balance sheet and were covered by provisions that were never above 15%. The regulations also allowed lender-financed interest payments to be recognized as income. The substandard category was widely used to paper over large impaired loans made to property developers.

It was at this time that Caja Castilla la Mancha failed spectacularly, the first of the Spanish savings banks to go, bringing down with it the whole edifice described above and triggering new measures.

5.4   Second Stage: The FROB and Institutional Protection Schemes

The Orderly Bank Restructuring Fund (Fondo de Reestructuración Ordenada de la Banca or 'FROB') was created by the Spanish government on the advice of private consultants. The institution was set up in mid-2009, and began its operations towards the end of the year with an initial endowment of €9 billion. Two years had passed since the onset of the crisis.

This new institution was to be the linchpin of the restructuring process in the savings banks. FROB would finance mergers between the *cajas de ahorros* using taxpayers' money to clean up their balance sheets and slash the number of institutions operating in the market, at the same time downsizing a bloated workforce and closing down unneeded branch offices. It was also the route chosen to convert the *cajas* gradually into banks via a series of legislative provisions.

The three deposit guarantee funds were merged into one, which survived as a single fund financed entirely by the Spanish financial system, and would henceforth play a residual role in the shadow of FROB. However, the new Deposit Guarantee Fund eventually had to act in the cases of Caja Castilla la Mancha (CCM), Caja de Ahorros del Mediterráneo (CAM) and UNNIM, in the latter two instances because FROB lacked the funds needed to bail out the institutions in question, obliging it to offer buyers asset protection schemes or 'APS' (or EPAs, Esquema de Protección de Activos) to underwrite a high proportion of as yet unrecognized losses at the time of purchase. These APSs would seriously eat into the guarantee fund's assets.

FROB's role, meanwhile, was to arrange mergers between the savings banks through institutional protection schemes (IPS), a newly created regulatory arrangement. Based on a questionable similarity with a German institution, IPSs were pushed, not to say imposed, by the Bank of Spain and its consultants on a case-by-case basis, supposedly acting as a form of gradual merger in commercial and accounting terms, so that they became known as 'cold mergers'.

To begin with, the member savings banks of each IPS would create a management company, which would handle loan arrangement and risk control for all. The IPSs also mutualized an initial 20% of capital and earnings, although this proportion was gradually raised to 100%. Driven by a succession of legislative provisions, the IPSs would then gradually be reshaped into banks. Each *caja de ahorros* thus endured on paper while their regulatory capital needs were fictitiously covered as a group, even if no group formally existed in legal terms.

The system was crippled by its own inherent defects from the outset:

- In accordance with the FROB's own regulations and the demands of the European authorities, the member savings banks of each IPS could receive government aid only if they were 'fundamentally sound'. However, this condition was never fulfilled as there were so few healthy *cajas* in the system. The result was that low-quality institutions, often still controlled at arm's length by regional governments of one or another political stripe, were grouped together into new institutions that were as artificial as they were weak.

- The Bank of Spain resorted in most cases to auditors and consultants to carry out the viability studies required before the formation of each IPS, but their recommendations were often wrong, and some resulted in mergers that were ill-starred from the outset. The Bank of Spain itself then formulated its own diagnoses of each unit in order to quantify the capital that FROB would have to provide, which it did by subscribing preference shares, that is, hybrid debt instruments, a questionable form of capital in my opinion.

In its diagnoses, the Bank of Spain placed the onus for the initial recapitalization of the savings banks on FROB, but the amounts required proved manifestly insufficient given the overly optimistic assumptions made about the value of assets and the scale of losses. No consideration was given to the lack of provisions to cover hidden losses, which immediately eroded capital. However, fictitious underlying gains on assets were taken into account in the computation of capital, together with good will, artificial assets revaluations, deferred tax credits and estimates of possible synergies.

The capitalization process was undertaken by transforming conventional deposits into regulatory capital instruments, principally preference shares. This was to become one of the most controversial issues of the crisis, because the savings banks' own commercial strength and the high yields paid on these securities (in many cases as much as 7%) made it easy to sell them to a financially illiterate clientele who largely lacked the expertise to comprehend the risks with which they were dealing.

The result was that the subscription of preference shares by FROB proved insufficient to restructure the IPSs and turn them into viable entities. The new institutions were simply allowed to stagger on for a few years, despite scarce capital and deep underlying losses which moreover increased over time, due both to the inertia of management and to the ongoing cost of maintaining non-productive assets financed by onerous liabilities without writing down their value or making proper provision.

We may note here that FROB did appoint new directors in the new IPS banks at this time, but their mandates were limited and they still had to work alongside some managers and executives of the former *cajas*. Despite the arrival of these new directors, then, the necessary changes to foster transparency, asset remuneration and reasonable management remuneration simply did not happen.

While the general IPS arrangements were still under way, the Spanish government found itself forced to address urgent cases like those of CCM, CAM and UNIM. These institutions were granted significant cash aid and efforts were made to secure their sale to other entities for a token price in return for taking on all initial known losses via the acquisition of preference shares.

It was at this time that the 'APS' or 'asset protection scheme' I mentioned above was created. In the absence of any reliable diagnosis at the time of the sale, the Deposit Guarantee Fund (FGD in the Spanish acronym) and FROB underwrote a significant percentage of any contingent or new losses that might arise for the buyers of the target institutions. Except in the case of CCM, this significant equity support was not accompanied by any cash injection, but was structured simply as a financial guarantee, the existence of which nonetheless allowed its beneficiaries to recognize gains in their books equal to the value of the APS granted. But with no cash.

5.5   Third Stage: 2012. A Change of Strategy

It was only in 2012, five years into the crisis, that the approach taken to the restructuring of the financial sector began clearly to change. This was a highly positive development, but it was not enough. At odds with the Bank of Spain's strategy, the government directly demanded that banks make significant general provisions for their entire property loan portfolios. This move was based on fresh finance industry diagnoses prepared by the external consultant Oliver Wyman, which had been controversially retained by the Bank of Spain to do the work of its own inspectors. Its recommendations took shape in two Royal Decree Laws issued in February and June, the first of which required provisions of €50 billion and the second of €30 billion. The aim was to cover all losses on outstanding property loans, as of 31 December 2011, through charges to the financial statements of 31 December 2012.

Meanwhile, the Spanish government entered into a memorandum of understanding, or MoU, with the troika in July 2012, bowing to pressure from the IMF, which had spent several months of that year making its own assessment of the Spanish finance industry. This deal allowed Spain to obtain a gigantic credit facility of €100 billion under very favourable terms from the European Stability Mechanism (ESM). In exchange, it agreed at last to use actual cash funds to recapitalize various merged savings banks, which had already been converted into banks. Bankia was the highest profile case, although the cases of Catalunya Bank and Abanca (created by the previous merger of saving banks of Catalonia and Galicia) were also significant.

The MoU also required the creation of a 'bad bank', SAREB, the asset management entity charged with the task of scouring the balance sheets of ailing banks to remove all of their impaired property assets. In order to capitalize Bankia, Catalunya Bank and Abanca and to fund SAREB's starting capital, the Spanish government, acting through FROB, would draw down €41.3 billion out of the €100 billion facility.

The losses existing in the banks earmarked for recapitalization were first recalculated in order to ensure realistic restructuring, which multiplied the amounts estimated when the IPSs were formed by 4 or 5 times.

6   The Case of Bankia

Bankia was born out of a cold merger between seven former savings banks based in disparate regions of Spain. The two largest of the merged institutions, Caja Madrid and Bancaja, were among the most problematic cases facing the country. Meanwhile, the IPS as a whole was burdened by huge unrecognized losses but had scant equity. Its actual net asset value was unknown.

Various measures were adopted to correct this decapitalization, although they would soon be replaced by others:

- In 2010, seven savings banks created an IPS, resulting in the creation of a bank (BFA) with capital of just €18 million in December of the same year. The new institution received an injection of capital via preference shares subscribed by FROB for a total of €4.47 billion.
- At that time, the total equity of the IPS' seven-member savings banks was €15.41 billion, while their recognized losses were €9.21 billion (around 60% of equity). These losses were charged against reserves and not through profit and loss.
- In February 2011, the Spanish government approved a Royal Decree Law, which lowered the capital requirement from 10% to 8% for listed banks. As of that moment, Bankia's seven-member savings banks focused single-mindedly on the goal of a stock market listing.
- To this end, each of the savings banks sold all of their assets and liabilities to BFA, the bank they had jointly created. BFA in turn sold the best quality assets and liabilities to another group bank, Altae, which then changed its name to Bankia. Bankia's shares were still held by BFA however, forming a consolidated group. Bankia was the institution that would seek to raise capital by offering new shares in the market.

- The assets and liabilities sold by the savings banks to BFA and then assigned to Bankia were appraised by private consultants, who estimated value at a little over € 20 billion. However, their work was not verified by the auditors.
- In June 2011, Bankia increased its share capital by more than €3 billion, representing some 48% of total capital. The price of the issue was €3.75 for each new share, just one-third of the book value of the old shares. Some consider that the network of Bankia was deeply negative at that time.
- The capital increase was sold to both retail and institutional investors under enormous pressure, though not necessarily from the market. Indeed, some of the institutions concerned lost little time in offloading the shares they had subscribed.
- The first warning of what was to come in Bankia occurred just three months after its stock market listing. In November 2011, the Bankia group requested the Bank of Spain to place Banco de Valencia, in which it held a stake of close to 40%, under administration. The Bank of Spain quickly agreed. Banco de Valencia was the first bank to be nationalized in the crisis, and also the first listed institution to suffer that fate, because its parent, Bankia, was unable to rescue it alone. On the contrary, Bankia simply turned its back on its affiliate and left the mess to the Spanish government via FROB, which proceeded to sell the moribund entity to Caixabank after a rescue costing €5.5 billion. This aid was not, then, destined for Bankia but rather to write off the losses of one of its affiliates, clearly flagging the Bankia group's overall weakness.
- The decrees issued by the new Spanish government also required all banks to submit plans to the Bank of Spain in April 2012 outlining how they proceed with the write-downs and provisions required. Bankia estimated that it would need to write off somewhat more than €7 billion. The Bank of Spain approved the plan designed by Bankia, although apparently subject to certain conditions. Meanwhile, the auditors who had certified the financial statements as of 31 December 2010, which Bankia had used to obtain its stock market listing in July 2011, suddenly baulked at signing the audit report on the 2011 accounts. The Spanish National Securities Market Commission (CNMV) then demanded that the group submit its audited financial statements. On 4 May, Bankia filed its unaudited financial statements for 2011 and management report, which showed a profit of €307 million in Bankia and losses of €30 million in its parent, BFA.
- After announcing the distribution of dividends on 7 May, Bankia suddenly informed the CNMV in a relevant event notice that its chairman had

resigned. He would be replaced by José Ignacio Goirigolzarri, who brought his own team with him.

- These were days of maximum uncertainty. Bankia's stock plunged and the CNMV finally suspended trading on 25 May 2012, by which time the price had dropped to €1.57 per share, less than half of the issue price paid by subscribers in the IPO less than a year earlier. In these circumstances, Bankia's new board decided:

  • to restate the financial statements presented 20 days earlier by the former management team, bringing to light significant losses both in BFA and in Bankia, which completely reversed the profits reported previously; and
  • to seek further assistance of €19 billion from the Spanish government for the BFA-Bankia group as a whole. Some €12 billion of this aid would be used for Bankia itself.

- Though it far exceeded the €7 billion estimated by Bankia's former management, this fresh injection of aid was approved by both the Spanish and European supervisory authorities. Meanwhile, the €4.47 billion in BFA preference shares subscribed by FROB in December 2010 would be converted into capital, adding to the €3 billion raised in the 2011 capital increase.
- In total, the Spanish government would provide total financial aid of €23.47 billion to capitalize the BFA-Bankia group, which had been considered 'fundamentally solvent' just eighteen months earlier.
- As a result of these transactions, FROB gained a significant presence both as a shareholder and on the board, which it retains to this day, since the group has not yet been sold, as required by the MoU.
- In addition to the €23.5 billion injected by FROB, the group also benefited from government guarantees which may not have required any cash outlay but nonetheless represented a significant risk for the Treasury. These guarantees covered the bonds received by Bankia from SAREB (€22.32 billion) by way of payment for its property assets and most of its deferred tax assets (€6.96 billion).
- The group also benefitted from the substantial guarantees granted by the Spanish government to underwrite securities issues in the early years of the crisis, although these did not finally result in any cost because the issuer (Bankia) paid the debts concerned on maturity.
- This successful but costly rescue of the seven saving banks' merger also involved key changes to the group's management, always essential together with recapitalization to achieve a positive outcome. The alternative would have been to allow the Bankia group to fail with unpredictable consequences.

7   SAREB

As agreed in the MoU, the Spanish government created a 'bad bank', SAREB, which was incorporated as a mixed limited liability company to acquire the worst of the intervened banks' and savings banks' property assets as a part of their restructuring. The idea was good, though the capital structure employed was poorly balanced. Moreover, the high book values of the majority of the assets acquired would complicate liquidation.

SAREB was conceived as a supplementary instrument for the recapitalization of the Spanish banking system. Its starting capital was €300 million with a share premium of €900 million, which was split between FROB (45%) and 21 private organizations (16 banks, 4 insurance companies and one power utility), which were 'invited' to acquire stakes by the Spanish government in an exercise of moral suasion. These shareholders, and a further five insurers, also subscribed some €3.6 billion of subordinated debt. SAREB then proceeded to acquire assets from the savings banks using these funds and the proceeds of a €51 billion bond issue backed by the Spanish government. The assets acquired consisted of repossessed properties (€11 billion), mortgage loans (€40 billion) and some non-performing unsecured loans (€1.9 billion).

However, SAREB's financial structure was imbalanced. Since its all of its assets were by definition problematic but purchased at above the market price—so that they generated only nugatory returns and would clearly be difficult to convert into cash—it may have been better to have aligned liabilities, and in particular the interest rate paid on the government-backed bonds, with the return on assets.

However, the SAREB bonds were initially offered to the market at a rate of interest linked to EURIBOR plus a spread, which was between 1.24% and 2.96% at the time of issue. A further benefit for purchasers was that the bonds could be presented to the ECB for rediscounting.

SAREB's assets were also singular. To begin with, the properties and claims acquired from the savings banks were not recognized at their market value at the date of purchase (late 2012 and early 2013), but rather at an 'average price' calculated by the consultancy Oliver Wyman, which was retained at the proposal of the troika.

This meant that the best assets were understated and the worst were overstated. The measurement of the assets in this way meant that all of the overstated assets would have to be provided for in the first year. In these circumstances, SAREB applied to the Spanish Institute of Accounting and Auditing (ICAC) for a special dispensation, which was eventually approved by the Bank of Spain. SAREB therefore applies unique accounting rules, which allow it not to recognize losses on its assets at the end of each year, but to treat them as offset by the theoretical underlying gains on other assets calculated based on external appraisals. Furthermore, the new accounting rules allowed SAREB significantly to increase the book value of its assets, but this makes their sale even more difficult.

In May 2013, SAREB entered into a swap contract to hedge the risk of a possible rise in the Euribor rate. This was the largest financial derivative that had ever been arranged in Europe until then. The swap was instrumented by a group of four banks, two of them significant shareholders of SAREB themselves. However, the losses incurred on this contract (€1.99 billion in December 2016) ate so far into SAREB's initial capital that it had to write down the total and capitalize a part of the subordinated debt issued (€2.17 billion).

Meanwhile, the IMF had demanded that SAREB be set up without delay, and this haste hindered proper identification and documentation of a part of the assets acquired. Hence, they could not be put up for sale and liquidation until the wearisome task of regularization was complete.

In short, SAREB's final total assets at the end of 2016 (€44.09 billion) were worth less than its liabilities (€46.75 billion).

By late 2017, SAREB had succeeded in liquidating one-fourth of its assets, probably the best ones, leaving it with three-fourths still to go, probably the worst. Any losses which may henceforth be incurred on the liquidation of these assets will be added to the operating losses arising from the unproductive nature of SAREB's assets and its significant costs, which comprise basically general and administrative expenses maintenance costs, significant marketing costs, and the interest and fees arising from the bad bank's financial structure. The outlook contrasts sharply with the 14% annual return anticipated upon SAREB's incorporation.

Turning to SAREB's impact on the restructured savings banks, the fact that the purchase price paid for their assets was calculated as an average between their net book value and alleged long-run value meant that the *cajas* were still left holding unrecognized losses.

8   Banco Popular

The recent episode involving the failure of Banco Popular deserves special mention as the first case of resolution under the new European Banking Union mechanisms. Given the fog that still surrounds this case, I will confine myself here to outlining the key events and raising some pertinent questions.

Banco Popular was for many years one of the world's most profitable banks. It was, in fact, widely held up as a model until the early 2000s, and it had been audited by Price Waterhouse since the 1980s, that is, for about 35 years.

Coinciding with most relevant changes in its top management, the bank began to grow rapidly in the latter 2000s, entering the real estate sector late but with lots of borrowed cash and a large appetite for risk, in both cases above the average for the industry. In fact, it appeared to be picking up some of the deals from which other banks were looking to withdraw.

After the crisis hit, Banco Popular adopted a rather lax policy with respect to the classification of assets and provisions for losses, perhaps because it was unable at once to set aside the full volume needed. This happened year after year.

In 2011, Banco Popular acquired Banco Pastor, with the encouragement of the Bank of Spain, according to market rumours. Given the weakness of the target bank, this deal may have aggravated Banco Popular's own fragile condition. It would certainly also have complicated supervision and clouded the transparency of the two banks. However, the transaction provided Banco Popular with very substantial (though equally questionable) goodwill, which it assigned to cover both probable and actual losses.

The bank also increased share capital twice, in 2012 and 2016, receiving some €5.5 billion from shareholders in just four years, though the resulting disbursements were partly financed by Banco Popular itself. However, it continued to hold a significant volume of non-productive assets, which it had not written down or provided for. These assets thus caused recurring losses and creeping decapitalization. These losses continued to eat away at its capital and cash flows until the events of 2017.

Something quite untoward happened in 2017. Having installed a new chairman, Banco Popular declared, in its first quarter report filed with the CNMV on 4 May, that its regulatory capital ratio was above 11% and that the business outlook was highly positive. These figures were not questioned by external auditors or the supervisory authorities at any level.

Just one month later, however, the bank was 'resolved' under the Single Resolution Mechanism (SRM), and FROB instrumented its sale to Banco Santander for a price of €1 after the overnight write-down of all its shares, plus subordinated debt for a total of some €2 billion. The decision was adopted urgently in view of the collapse in the bank's share price, which may have been triggered by hazy manipulations but was certainly fuelled by market unease and, above all, by the abrupt withdrawal of deposits following leaks from various sources, some of them perhaps institutional. The run on deposits compounded Banco Popular's increasing liquidity problems, which were in turn caused by increasing decapitalization.

It was this illiquidity that finally triggered the bank's resolution. Nevertheless, the root cause was Banco Popular's gradual decapitalization over a period of some years, even though the process might not have yet consumed all of its capital. How could this happen?

To begin with, it is very difficult for any analyst to comprehend how the bank's managers could live with the constant deterioration of its equity without taking any measures; how the Spanish supervisory authorities could have failed to identify these problems or to take energetic and effective corrective action; or, indeed, how the external auditors could have gone on issuing their clean reports for years. Likewise, one can only wonder what was the nature of the supervision afforded by the all-powerful Single Supervisory Mechanism created as part of the European Banking Union over the period of almost three years in which it was responsible for Banco Popular.

Furthermore, all of these events were justified by the as yet undisclosed diagnoses prepared post haste by an external auditor (Deloitte) and not by supervisors at the Bank of Spain, who appear to have been left entirely in the dark.

9   The Cost to the Taxpayer

In September 2017, the Bank of Spain published an information notice on the government aid contributed to resolve the recent crisis. In it, the Bank confirmed that public rescues had required the disbursement of capital for a total of €64.30 billion, two-thirds of which consisted of direct aid granted to FROB and one-third of assistance for Spain's Deposit Guarantee Fund, which is to say the financial industry itself.

Meanwhile, the Asset Protection Schemes guaranteed a large part of the potential losses which might arise for the new owners of the savings banks following their acquisition. These guarantees were also split between FROB and the Deposit Guarantee Fund (FGD), and their final cost will only be known after all of the related transactions are settled.

The losses that are likely to arise under the guarantees granted to back all of the SAREB bond issues, which currently total some €40.93 billion, could also result in a considerable cost for the public purse.

Finally, the Spanish government also granted guarantees backing deferred tax assets (DTAs) for an initial total of €44 billion against a fee. The majority of the DTAs guaranteed (or 'monetized') consisted of tax losses incurred by insolvent institutions, which thus became a tax exemption at the cost of the Treasury.

The cost of this aid to the taxpayer can be calculated by deducting the amounts granted from possible recoveries by government, obtained in the form of proceeds from the future sale of all or part of its shareholdings in entities like Bankia, dividends received by FROB from the institutions in which it holds shares, the portion of bad real estate assets purchased by SAREB and fee income earned by the government on the guarantees granted in respect of the DTA and the debt issued by the restructured financial institutions, SAREB bonds. It will therefore not be possible to calculate the final net cost to the taxpayer until the settlement of these operations, although it is foreseeable that the amount will be large.

In any event, the corporate income tax which the government will obtain from formerly loss-making but now restructured and profitable financial institutions should also be taken into account in this context.

Whatever the final result, it is clear that the Spanish government's handling of the crisis proved very costly for taxpayers, as it also was for the financial system itself via the Deposit Guarantee Fund, although to a lesser extent.

These costs are clearly greater than they would have been had the authorities taken prompt and effective early action. Moreover, the purpose of the aid granted was to compensate the institutions that took over the ailing banks and savings banks for the losses they took on and for the burden of managing the restructuring process.

It is unfortunate that the taxpayer should have had to foot so large a bill for the restructuring of the savings banks, and it was in this light that the recent EU legislation provided for the bail-in mechanism, by which it would be the shareholders and the creditors of an insolvent bank who would pay for its rescue rather than government. The object is to prevent private sector problems from spilling over into the public sector. It is to be hoped that this new mechanism will work, in spite of the problems it may cause in the market.

The private sector is also asked to contribute to rescues via guarantee schemes, which could be utilized to a greater or lesser extent depending on the applicable legislation and the circumstances.

Should the closure of insolvent financial institutions be considered the ideal option? In the case of Bankia and the other Spanish savings banks, closure would have resulted in nationwide collapse, disrupting the payments system and resulting in systemic contagion of the broader economy and jobs.

Let us make a brief digression here. Which supervisors were the most successful in rescuing their financial systems in the crisis, and what did they gain in terms of the recovery of the funds applied? The answer is those who were quick to restructure using large dollops of taxpayers' money to ensure a definitive solution to problems. The US is a clear example.

In this light, we may wonder whether the fiscal cost of rescues should without exception be treated as taboo, or whether it would not be better to entertain the possibility of effective government participation in rescue operations, alongside other mechanisms. Incomplete solutions are almost always the dearest. It might also be wise to review all of the sometimes-questionable post-crisis legislation enacted, the unequal supervision provided by the Single Supervisory Mechanism in its present form, and the still immature resolution mechanism established as part of the European Banking Union.

10   The Situation Today (December 2017)

10.1   Positive Aspects

The system as a whole has clearly improved after the last 10 years of crisis, and this process has had its positive aspects as well as its faults.

- The financial system was bloated, and it has been successfully slimmed down by over one-third in terms of the number of bank branches and employees, which may be similar to the proportion by which it had swelled during the bubble.
- The new banks resulting from the mergers of the insolvent *cajas de ahorros* were acquired overall by more solvent, better managed organizations.
- Meanwhile, most of the surviving *cajas* have become full-fledged banks and exist now only as minority shareholders of these new institutions but without any banking business of their own. It only remains, then, to limit their influence in their new role as shareholders of their affiliated banks.
- The political influence formerly wielded by regional governments and non-professional directors has been to a great extent rolled back.

Nevertheless, numerous problems remain, and they are at the root of the current low profitability in the financial industry. What are the causes?

- Significant volumes of non-performing assets remain on the banks' balance sheets, hindering the generation of positive cash flows and causing additional current losses. This problem is at the heart of the low return on assets now observable in the financial sector as a whole.
- Interest rates remain very low as a result of the ECB's monetary policy.
- The overall volume of credit remains below pre-crisis levels as a result of the two-thirds contraction in the worst years of the crisis.

- Earnings have suffered, then, and will continue to do so despite the efficiency gains achieved as a result of mergers and the wave of digitization currently in progress, especially in larger organizations.

Low returns are compounded by significant instability.

- The surplus liquidity existing in the markets, at very low interest rates, which the ECB continues to stimulate, clouds managers' judgement and blurs their sense of risk. It is also a prime cause of bubbles, which end by bursting. It also leads banks to enter higher risk operations.
- Finally, there is the issue of deregulation announced in the US, which may force European banking to tread a similar path in order to stay competitive.
- Moreover, unregulated banking (shadow banking and online banking) continue to gain ground over conventional retail banking.
- These problems exist in the context of what was initially perceived as the great panacea, namely, the European Banking Union based on the twin pillars of the Single Supervisory Mechanism and the Single Resolution Mechanism, but in the absence of any guarantee scheme. Furthermore, while the new European banking regulations demand more capital (though of a somewhat questionable nature), it largely ignores quantitative supervision and preventive and prompt restructuring of banks' balance sheets. Compounded by divergences between accounting and prudential rules, which will generate confusion and may hinder the work of auditors and supervisors alike.
- To cap it all, the world has entered a period of geopolitical instability in key strategic areas, both internationally and within some nation states.

11   Conclusions

Megamergers designed to create systemic banks that are 'too big to fail' cannot be recommended as a solution to the problems of the financial industry. This is because, they are extraordinarily difficult to manage and can present an obstacle to effective supervision, and because the resolution of such entities is impossible in practice, which is a serious hazard.

In spite of everything, if we can follow up on the positive outcomes achieved by some of the measures already taken by avoiding complacency, completing all of the remaining restructuring processes, strengthening credit management, actively seeking further efficiency gains and encouraging transparency in the markets, then we may view the future of the financial system in a more optimistic light. But not otherwise.

Index

A

Accordion, 25, 83
Adjusted accounts, 24, 54
Any loss is a good loss, 112
Asset bubbles, 88, 118
Asset classification and provisioning,
    44, 53
Asset valuation, xvi, 98, 99, 116–118
Audit, xii, 6, 12, 24, 25, 46, 70, 92,
    104, 105, 117, 135
Auditors, 13, 24, 46, 53, 65, 67–71, 73,
    92, 98, 99, 104, 105, 123, 128,
    130, 132, 135, 139, 140, 143
Avoiding complacency, 143

B

Bad bank, xvi, 2, 85, 110, 111, 118,
    119, 130, 134, 137, 138
Bail-ins, 90, 92, 108–110, 141
Banco de Valencia, 135
Banco Pastor, 139
Bank crisis, xi, xv, xvii, 14, 17–29,
    31–39, 90, 126, 130

Bank mergers, 47
Bank of Spain, x, xi, xv–xix, 18, 19,
    21–25, 27–29, 32, 82–84, 128,
    130–133, 135, 137, 139, 140
Bank restructuring, 23, 42, 46, 64,
    68, 130
Basel II, 79, 80, 91
Basel III, 91, 102
Basel IV, 91, 106
Black holes, 96, 108
Burden-sharing, 109

C

The CAMEL system, 2
Capital, xi–xiii, xvii, xix, 2, 22, 33, 41,
    69, 79, 87, 98, 115, 125
Capital components, 88, 92
The case of Bankia, 142–143
Cash flows, xiii, 9, 11, 47–49, 53, 55,
    58, 98, 100, 103, 108, 118,
    139, 142
Changing the management team,
    50, 85

© The Author(s) 2019
A. de Juan, *From Good to Bad Bankers*,
https://doi.org/10.1007/978-3-030-11551-7

The closure of insolvent financial
   institutions, 141
Compliance, 3, 13, 14, 21, 39, 44, 45,
   56, 70, 97, 106, 117
Concentration, 4–6, 10, 13, 18, 27,
   34–36, 71, 96, 101, 127
Consolidation, 44, 101
Contingent convertible bonds (CoCos),
   88, 101, 117, 139
Convertible securities, 101
Cosmetic accounts, 54
Cosmetic management, 7–9, 11, 13
The cost to the taxpayer, 142–143
Credit facility of €100 billion, 133

D

Debt for equity swaps, 50
Decapitalization, 88, 104, 107, 118,
   134, 139, 140
Delay, 61, 85, 89, 128, 138
Deposit Guarantee Fund, 21–23, 131,
   133, 140, 141
Deregulation, 2, 37, 69, 116,
   124–126, 143
Desperate management, 3, 7, 10–11, 13
Desperate measures, xi, 96
Developers, 124, 130
Dividends, 3, 6–8, 10, 50, 54, 55,
   63, 68, 79, 98, 111, 117, 121,
   135, 141

E

The ethics of restructuring, 67–75
European Banking Union, xviii, 51,
   87–90, 92, 138, 140, 142, 143
Evergreening, xii, 8, 9, 70, 97, 120
Excess liquidity, xii, xviii, 95, 96,
   116, 119
Expected losses, 92, 100, 101,
   119, 120
External roadblocks, 128

F

The failure of Banco Popular, 138
Failure of political will, 62, 64, 70
False friends, 41–51, 118
Financial deregulation, 124, 125
Financial engineering, 58, 102,
   118, 119
Fiscal discipline, 58–60
Fit and proper, xiii, 4, 126
Fondo de Reestructuración Ordenada
   de la Banca (FROB), 130–137,
   139–143
Forbearance, 98, 103, 106, 118
A forward-looking approach, 115, 118
Fraud, xi, xvii, 3, 11–14, 36, 37,
   45, 63, 72, 73, 107, 111,
   112, 127

G

The general failure to react, 142–143
Geopolitical instability, 116, 143
Geopolitical uncertainties, 93
Good governance, 89, 92, 104
Good will, 88, 101, 132
Governance, ix, xiii, 82, 92, 106, 118
Growth, xii, xviii, 4, 6, 11, 33, 34, 37,
   48, 59, 60, 78, 79, 85, 96, 107,
   125–127

H

Handling of the crisis, 127–129, 141
Hole, 14, 58, 118, 122
Hypothetical stability, 116

I

IAS 39, 128
Illiquidity, 3, 11, 15, 34, 36, 37, 64,
   68, 125, 140
Income recognition, 53, 99–100, 119
Incompetence, 69, 96

Incomplete solutions, 142
Increased share capital, 139
Incurred losses, 119, 128
Ineffective supervision, 2, 36, 96
Insolvency, xi–xiii, xvii–xx, 3, 7, 13–15,
    22, 23, 25, 32, 34, 36–38, 42,
    44–48, 50, 51, 53–56, 58, 59,
    61, 63, 64, 68, 73, 90, 92,
    95–98, 104, 106–109, 118,
    125, 128, 129
Insolvency and foreclosure, 61
Inspection, 45, 54, 89, 103, 117, 118,
    120–122
International bubble, 124–125
International Financial Reporting
    Standard (IFRS), 9, 100, 119
Intrusive supervision, 93, 115

L

Legacy, xi, xv, xvi, 48, 93
Legal uncertainty, 60–61
Lessons to be learned, 2, 14–15
Levels of estimated losses, 98
Leverage ratio, 92, 102
Liquidation of bad assets, 73, 85, 122
Liquidity and Euphoria, 77–80
Liquidity difficulties, 10, 11, 22
Liquidity support, 47, 48, 64, 118

M

Macroeconomics factors, 1, 32
Macro prudential supervision, 102
Malpractice, 14, 63, 70–75, 84, 97,
    106, 107, 111, 118, 127
Management, ix–xii, xv, xvii, 1–4, 6–7,
    12–16, 22, 25–28, 31–33, 37–39,
    42, 47, 50, 51, 58, 61, 63, 69, 70,
    75, 82–85, 89, 95–99, 106, 107,
    110–112, 117, 121, 126, 129,
    131, 132, 134–136, 139, 143

Management culture deterioration, 12
Manipulation, 7, 102, 121, 139
Market access, 43
Megamergers, 143
Memorandum of understanding, 133
Mergers, 42, 47, 54, 78, 79, 81, 85, 93,
    108, 109, 128, 131–134, 136,
    142, 143
The microeconomic roots, 31–39
Mismatch, 5, 34, 37, 96
Modelling, xii, 89, 105
Models, xi, 1, 2, 7, 21, 39, 53, 54, 56,
    90, 92, 100, 103, 105, 106,
    117–120, 130, 139
Monetary expansion, 93, 108,
    116, 118
Money hose, 129–130
Moral hazard, xviii, 58, 59, 62–65,
    108, 112, 118, 121
The most successful in rescuing, 141

N

New management, x, 12, 25, 82, 83
Non-performing assets, 10, 54, 55, 59,
    98, 116, 119, 120, 137
Non-performing loans (NPL), xii, xix,
    44, 115–122, 129
No supervision, 103, 121

O

Obstacles to crisis resolution, 57–65
On-site, case-by-case inspection, 120
On-site verification, 103, 106
Other people's money, 34, 37, 72
The overall volume of credit, 142
Overextension, 4, 13, 33, 34
Owners, boards and managers, 108
Ownership, xi, 4, 5, 7, 12, 22, 24, 25,
    28, 42, 47, 61, 73–75, 82, 111,
    112, 128

P

Paying for a funeral, 116
Political will, 48, 54, 62, 64, 70, 117,
    128, 129
Poor credit policy, 34
Poor lending, 4, 38, 96
Practical lessons, xix
Preference shares, 132–134, 136
Preventive medicine, 88
Privatization, 42, 50, 51, 78
Problem banks, 16, 17, 22, 24, 36, 39,
    48–50, 53, 95, 98, 100, 103,
    108, 110, 112, 116, 120, 122
Property, 10, 68, 71, 93, 123–125,
    127, 128, 130, 133, 134,
    136, 137
Property appraisers, 123
Provisions, xiii, 8, 9, 13–15, 36, 41, 44,
    49, 50, 53–55, 63, 70, 71, 79,
    83, 98–101, 117, 120–122, 127,
    130–133, 135, 139

R

Rating agencies, 53, 65, 123, 124
Real capital, 48, 58, 100, 101, 108,
    117, 118
The real cash flow, 10, 103, 108
Recapitalization, 39, 47–51, 64, 83,
    108–110, 132, 134, 136, 137
Recognition of accruals, 9, 13
Refinance, 48, 70, 97
Regulation, x, xii, xvi, xvii, 2, 3, 6, 13,
    14, 18, 32, 39, 41–45, 51, 60,
    62–65, 68, 70, 88–90, 92, 95,
    99–103, 105, 116, 119, 120,
    130, 131, 143
Rehabilitation, 21, 23, 24, 27, 28
Related-party, 34, 36, 38, 97
Relying on growth, 107
Relying on time, 96, 107

Reschedule, 8, 49
Rescue, ix, x, xvi, 63, 73, 74, 82, 85,
    109, 111, 119, 122, 135, 136,
    140–142
Resolution, ix, xi, xii, xvi, 16, 46,
    51, 56–65, 92, 93, 95, 99,
    101, 103, 107, 118, 119,
    122, 128, 129, 138, 140,
    142, 143
Return of assets, 97
Risk-weighted supervision (RWS), 101
Royal Decree Laws, 133, 134
The Rumasa case, 26–28

S

The sale of failed institutions, xvi, 83
Sampling mechanisms, 120
SAREB, 134, 136, 137, 140, 141
Savings banks, ix, xi, xvi, 18, 19,
    22, 81, 83, 84, 124–138,
    140, 141
Self-lending, 11, 72
The situation today, 142–143
Spanish banking crisis of the 1970s and
    80s, xvii, 15, 17–29, 36
Specific provisions, 100, 121
Speculation, 10, 12, 35, 71, 96, 125
Spiral, xi, 7, 14, 71, 96
Strengthen governance, 92–93
Stress test, xii, 89, 90, 92, 103, 106,
    117, 120
Sub-prime mortgages, 124
Substandard, 130
Supervision, xii, xiii, xvi, 1–3, 6, 7,
    13–14, 17, 32, 42, 43, 45–46,
    60, 63, 64, 68, 88, 89, 92, 93,
    95–100, 102–107, 112,
    115–121, 139, 140, 142, 143
Supervision of procedures, 106
Surgical measures, 83

T
Technical mismanagement, 3–6, 10
Tightening the screw, 119–120
Too big to fail, 61–62, 143
Transparency, 68–71, 79, 97, 100,
        104, 106, 118, 121, 129, 132,
        139, 143

U
The ultimate goal of resolution, 107
Undisclosed insolvency, 53–56, 98
Unrecognized losses, 131, 134, 138

Unregulated banking, 143
Unverified information, 117
Upside-down income statement, 7, 8
US Office of the Comptroller of the
        Currency, 32, 77

V
Vulnerability, 93

W
Weak recovery procedures, 38